W9-ABN-091

The New York Times

IN THE HEADLINES

Defining Sexual Consent

WHERE THE LAW FALLS SHORT

THE NEW YORK TIMES EDITORIAL STAFF

Published in 2019 by The New York Times® Educational Publishing
in association with The Rosen Publishing Group, Inc.
29 East 21st Street, New York, NY 10010

First Edition

The New York Times
Alex Ward: Editorial Director, Book Development
Phyllis Collazo: Photo Rights/Permissions Editor
Heidi Giovine: Administrative Manager

Rosen Publishing
Megan Kellerman: Managing Editor
Julia Bosson: Editor
Greg Tucker: Creative Director
Brian Garvey: Art Director

Cataloging-in-Publication Data
Names: New York Times Company.
Title: Defining sexual consent: where the law falls short / edited
by the New York Times editorial staff.
Description: New York : New York Times Educational Publishing,
2019. | Series: In the headlines | Includes glossary and index.
Identifiers: ISBN 9781642821093 (library bound) | ISBN
9781642821086 (pbk.) | ISBN 9781642821109 (ebook)
Subjects: LCSH: Sexual consent—Juvenile literature. | Sexual
ethics—Juvenile literature. | Rape—Juvenile literature.
Classification: LCC HQ32.D445 2019 | DDC 176'.4—dc23

Manufactured in the United States of America

On the cover: Illustration by Linda Huang.

Contents

CHAPTER 3

Looking for Solutions

CHAPTER 4

The Affirmative Consent Debate

CHAPTER 5

Key Cases

Introduction

IN THE FALL of 2014, Emma Sulkowicz, a senior at Columbia University, made headlines across the country with their thesis art project, "Carry That Weight." Mx. Sulkowicz, who uses nonbinary honorifics and pronouns, committed themself to carrying their 50-pound university-issue twin XL mattress around campus with them to all of their classes. The physical burden, they explained, represented the emotional difficulty they experienced as a survivor of sexual assault: the fall of their sophomore year, they had been sexually assaulted by a member of a fraternity. Columbia heard the case, but even after two other women came forward with their stories about the same student, the university panel dismissed the charges against him.

Sulkowicz's experience is representative of a larger crisis reaching its apex on university campuses. RAINN.org estimates that one out of four female undergraduates and one out of twenty male students experience a form of sexual violence. Over the years, university officials and police forces have done little to resolve or stem this epidemic. Sulkowicz's case helped to spark a debate that many saw as long overdue: What constitutes sexual consent? When can it be revoked? How can universities offer safety to their students inside their bedrooms? And how can these cases be litigated when the evidence comes down to two people's experiences of an intimate encounter, sometimes blurred by alcohol?

For the victims of sexual assault, the consequences can be traumatic. The number of sexual assaults reported on campuses greatly exceeds the number of students disciplined for committing them, and that fails to account for those that go unreported. In order to understand what is at stake in this debate, it is essential to listen to the first-person testimony provided by survivors. The articles in this book

Students at the Urban School of San Francisco attended a health class focused on affirmative consent in San Francisco, Oct. 1, 2015. With Gov. Jerry Brown's signature on a bill that month, California became the first state to require all high school health education classes give lessons on affirmative consent, which includes explaining that someone who is drunk or asleep cannot grant consent.

feature the voices of numerous victims of sexual assault and show the impact of these experiences on their university educations, psychological states and lives.

The debates over sexual assault tend to fall into two camps: while victims and victims' advocates see a system that creates an insurmountable burden of proof, the other side sees a process that presumes guilt before innocence and a campus mentality that resembles more of a witch hunt than a fair trial. Paul Nungesser, the student accused of assaulting Sulkowicz, won a lawsuit against Columbia University in 2017 claiming that the university failed to protect him from the consequences of Sulkowicz's project.

The articles in this book highlight the cases that pushed the debate over sexual consent into the headlines as well as the innovative solutions that have been proposed to address the issue of sexual assault. One policy that has emerged is the notion of affirmative consent: sexual encounters must involve both parties making explicit statements of their consent. In other words, while sexual consent has traditionally been taught as "no means no," universities that institute affirmative assent policies now show students that "yes means yes."

In order to put pressure on universities to step up their response systems to these situations, the Obama administration set new guidelines for universities to address the complaints on campus. However, in 2017, Betsy DeVos, President Trump's secretary of education, announced her plans to undo many of those protections, claiming that the policies did more to harm the accused than to protect the victims. And so the debate rages on. Meanwhile, individuals attempt to negotiate intimate relationships in the gray zone.

CHAPTER 1

Understanding Sexual Consent

The challenge in litigating sexual consent comes from its difficulty as an objective concept. Despite sexual education, consent remains difficult to talk about, both before and during sexual encounters. The articles in this chapter highlight the issues at stake in this debate: What constitutes consent? Who can give it? And can it be taken away? What constitutes rape and when is it miscommunication or, simply, bad sex?

Getting to 'No'

ESSAY | BY SUSAN DOMINUS | DEC. 21, 2014

THE NIGHT STARTED, as so many college nights do, with a red cup pressed into a hand. Ubiquitous at tail gates and parties, those bright plastic cups are a harbinger of carnival, of unleashing. The hand around the cup was mine.

I remember many of the details only vaguely, but the cup shines through; I can still taste the sweet-sour drink inside it. No matter how much I sipped — and each sip made the next one easier — the cup remained filled, courtesy of a young man, a fellow college senior, attending to its contents. I liked him, a little; I found his focus — on me — impressive.

I drank from the red cup, and in the next scene from that evening that I can recall, I am on my bed, and he is on top of me. I am resisting, but he is heavy, so heavy, and my limbs so leaden. I am certain he thought he was, as we used to say back then, a totally decent guy. Even now, I can imagine him as someone's loyal husband, a maker of pancakes, his kids' soccer coach. But that night I said no, and still he lay there, massive, pleading, sloppy with beer, for what seemed to be hours (but surely was not), until I finally stopped holding him off. Too close to sleep to rouse myself to outrage, I settled for capitulation, then revulsion.

In the past weeks, I have been thinking about that evening, its foggy events summoned by the two dozen or so women who bravely stepped forward to accuse Bill Cosby; by reports of sexual assaults on campuses; by a young woman at Columbia University so furious that she carries around a mattress in protest. All of this has jolted me, and other women, into a moment of openness, an openness that reveals not just a secret, but the secrecy itself. We would have thought ourselves too enlightened, too freed from a legacy of shame, to have hidden those complicated stories all these years. But some of us did. A woman I know recently told me about a sexual assault she endured in college; it was the first time she had spoken of it, she said, in 20 years, including many in therapy. I had never told anyone — not my husband, not my best friend and roommate at the time — about that particular night in college.

I have found myself having conversations with friends and female acquaintances and women I know only online, some of whom were painfully re-evaluating past experiences as sexual assault. But many conversations were attempts to make sense of encounters that fell, in our own minds, into some murky realm. There was no roofie, no pre-planned assault, nor, in some instances, were there protestations — but those encounters were upsetting nonetheless. One friend described a sexual experience, at 19, with a friend's much older brother: "In my head, I was trying to think of ways to get him to stop, and I couldn't, so I just lay there, paralyzed."

By the legal definition, what happened the night of the red cup was sexual assault: I said no. He pressured me, until, under the influence,

I stopped resisting. I can imagine other young women in similar situations justifiably going to their universities or pressing charges. But in the disgusted days that followed my own encounter, though I was angry, I did not consider myself the victim of an attack. If I had been afraid of anything, it was only of some deeply awkward moment. I did not have it in me to make a scene.

In 1993, one year after I graduated from college, Katie Roiphe published an incendiary op-ed in The New York Times called "Date Rape's Other Victim," in which she suggested that the issue of sexual assault on campus was overblown, that some feminists were casting women as passive victims in need of protection. She offered one way I could look at what happened to me that evening: "There is a gray area in which one person's rape may be another's bad night," she wrote. I was no ingénue, and had had "bad nights"; and yet the night of the red cup stood out as something significantly more troubling than that.

The language we use for a given experience inevitably defines how we feel about it. I could not land on language that felt right — to me — about that encounter. I still cannot.

Struggling to find language to define that experience after the fact left me longing for more words that could have been used in the moment. What I wish I had had that night was a linguistic rip cord, something without the mundane familiarity of "no" or the intensity demanded in "Get off or I'll scream."

"No" and "stop" — of course, they should be said and respected. But several women who told me they felt their consent was ambiguous said that in the moment, they froze, and language eluded them altogether: They said nothing. Because those words are inherently confrontational, they can require a degree of strength that someone who is feeling pressured or confused or is just losing her nerve or changing her mind might not have.

What if every kid on every college campus was given new language — a phrase whose meaning could not be mistaken, that signaled peril for both sides, that might be more easily uttered?

One phrase that might work is "red zone" — as in, "Hey, we're in a red zone," or "This is starting to feel too red zone." Descriptive and matter-of-fact, it would not implicitly assign aggressor and victim, but would flatly convey that danger — emotional, possibly legal — lay ahead. Such a phrase could serve as a linguistic proxy for confronting or demanding, both options that can seem impossible in the moment. "We're in a red zone" — the person who utters that is not a supplicant ("Please stop"); or an accuser ("I told you to stop!"). Many young women are uncomfortable in either of those roles; I know I was.

In an ideal world, clear consent will always precede sex, and young women (and men) who do find themselves in a tricky situation will express their discomfort firmly. But in the imperfect world in which we live, new language — if not red zone, then some other phrase that could take off with the universality of slang — might fill a silence.

Quite possibly no language would have worked for me that night: most men who do not heed no are not going to heed "red zone" either. But if such a phrase had existed, I think I would have reached for it: a quick, unemotional way to telegraph how deeply uncomfortable I was, without having to explain to someone I barely knew just how deeply uncomfortable I was. It is hard to talk about sex under the best of circumstances. I could not rise to the challenge of confrontation, much less frank talk, which required an intimacy that he and I did not share and that I had no interest in.

In the days following that encounter, I avoided calls from the guy, who so clearly misunderstood the situation that he thought he was courting me; there may have been flowers, but not to apologize. I considered him someone between a brute and an oaf, my own experience falling somewhere between assault and just a bad night. I never felt I was a victim; looking back, I was an English major for whom language failed at a moment when I needed it most.

The Challenge of Defining Rape

BY IAN URBINA | OCT. 11, 2014

LAST MONTH it was California, this month New York. States across the country are trying to figure out how to address the problem of sexual assault more effectively, and more often than not, they are looking to redefine the scope of sexual misconduct.

California's new law requires universities receiving state funding to switch from a "no means no" approach to a "yes means yes" standard, requiring partners to make an "affirmative, unambiguous and conscious decision" before having sex, and making clear that silence or a lack of resistance cannot be interpreted as consent. Gov. Andrew M. Cuomo of New York announced that the State University of New York would similarly define consent as an affirmative act on all its campuses, one that requires "clear, knowing and voluntary" participation.

With an effort also underway by the American Law Institute to reconsider when an assault becomes rape, some legal experts predict that changes to criminal laws in many states may not be far off.

As a social issue, sexual assault has seen a significant uptick in attention over the past year or so. There have been a flurry of federal actions, for example, aimed at countering rape in the military, prisons, immigration detention centers and on campuses.

But there is still little uniformity on how to define rape, which makes counting rapes, and countering and even discussing the issue, difficult. In many contexts, such as the major federal law on prison rape, "sexual assault" is used instead of "rape" because it covers nonconsensual acts like kissing and groping that fall short of many people's definition of actual rape. Until 2012, the Federal Bureau of Investigation still considered rape a crime committed solely against women, a definition that has since been expanded.

Over all, states have broadened the definition of rape and assault more than the federal government, according to a survey of the legal system conducted by AEquitas, a nonprofit group that provides prosecutors with resources on violence against women.

Clarifying consent is a common stumbling block. "Is the fact that the victim murmured, whispered, cried or moaned 'no' sufficient to establish nonconsent that a reasonable sexual partner should understand to be nonconsent?" asked Mary D. Fan, a professor at the University of Washington School of Law. The role of alcohol in rape cases is another subject of scrutiny, especially since drinking is often voluntary.

Stephen J. Schulhofer, a New York University law professor, said many states still require proof of physical aggression, though a growing number no longer do. Instead, they focus on the need for consent and therefore include situations such as assaults of people too intoxicated to give consent. Even so, most of these states do not specifically define genuine consent.

Some states, like New York, ask whether a reasonable person would believe that intercourse was consensual, considering all the surrounding circumstances. Meanwhile, some states follow the "no means no" rule, while others — including New Jersey — have adopted standards requiring affirmative, freely given permission by each person.

Last year, the definition issue came up when Washington State removed the spousal exemption clause from the definition of rape in the third degree, so that spouses are now deemed raped in cases of nonconsensual sex without forcible compulsion.

Definitions also depend partly on who is involved. In the case of statutory rape, for instance, some states set rules providing for a minimum age difference between partners. Other states do not.

In some parts of the country, not just force but resistance is required for an act to qualify as rape. In such cases, merely saying "no" would not in itself be considered sufficient resistance.

"Figuring out what to do with a verbal 'no' is still in many places a fraught idea, particularly where subsequent conduct suggests a possible change of heart," said Erin E. Murphy, a law professor at New York University.

The differing definitions can obscure how often rapes and sexual assaults are reported to authorities, said Corey Rayburn Yung, a law professor at the University of Kansas. Mr. Yung published a study in March that found that more than 796,000 rapes were not included in the F.B.I.'s tally between 1995 and 2012, partly because of the way the police handled cases in which the person who was assaulted did not meet the department's definition of a rape victim.

Definitions have also shifted dramatically over time. As recently as 40 years ago, no state allowed husbands to be prosecuted for raping their wives. Sixty years ago, in some Southern and Western states, sexual relations between a black man and a white woman could be considered rape. In 1998, Mississippi became the last state to drop a provision holding that statutory rape wasn't really rape if the girl was not of "chaste character."

Some legal scholars say that, in some cases, different definitions can be appropriate. Colleges, which aim to create environments where all students can be safe, are right to set codes of conduct defining rape more expansively than criminal laws that carry jail time, said Anne M. Coughlin, a law professor at the University of Virginia. The challenge, she said, is to ensure that everyone is aware of the distinctions. "We've seen cases where women have reported to off-campus police that they have been raped, only to learn that the criminal law doesn't extend to their case," she said. "That experience is really, really painful."

Professor Schulhofer of New York University, who is leading an effort by the American Law Institute to update the Model Penal Code, which is frequently cited as the standard for American state laws, sees an urgent need to codify national standards regarding rape and sexual assault. "The impetus for reform is not to achieve uniformity for its own sake," he said, "but rather to promote more just outcomes within individual states."

When Saying 'Yes' Is Easier Than Saying 'No'

BY JESSICA BENNETT | DEC. 16, 2017

FOR YEARS, my female friends and I have spoken, with knowing nods, about a sexual interaction we call "the place of no return." It is a kind of sexual nuance that most women instinctively understand: the situation you thought you wanted, or maybe you actually never wanted, but somehow here you are and it's happening and you desperately want out, but you know that at this point exiting the situation would be more difficult than simply lying there and waiting for it to be over. In other words: saying yes when we really mean no.

In my own life, I've had plenty of "no return" encounters, but there is one in particular that still makes me cringe. I was 19 and he was in his 30s, the older brother of a childhood classmate my friends and I fawned over as teenagers. I was home from college, old enough for him to notice, and he did, and then it was happening, and by then I was absolutely sure I didn't want it to happen, but in some combination of fear (that I wasn't as mature as he thought), shame (that I had let it get this far), and guilt (would I hurt his feelings?) I let it.

There are other names for this kind of sex: gray zone sex, in reference to that murky gray area of consent; begrudgingly consensual sex, because, you know, you don't really want to do it but it's probably easier to just get it over with; lukewarm sex, because you're kind of "meh" about it; and, of course, bad sex, where the "bad" refers not to the perceived pleasure of it, but to the way you feel in the aftermath.

It is also, as of last week, known as " 'Cat Person' sex," a reference to a short story published in The New Yorker that has sent a certain cohort of young people into fits.

Written by 36-year-old Kristen Roupenian, "Cat Person" is, by one interpretation, an utterly ordinary story of a modern-day sexual encounter between a woman and a man, in which text messages are

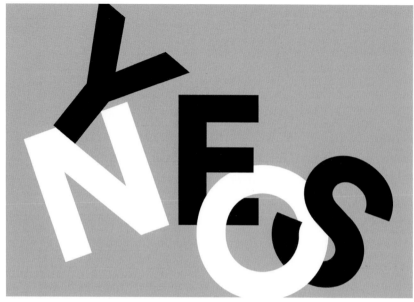

LINDA HUANG

exchanged and lukewarm sex is had; then she (spoiler alert) ghosts him, and he, desperate in his need to know why, calls her a "whore." It is not a story about consent, per se. But it is a window into the uncomfortable reality that clouds it.

The story most likely would have resonated with young women regardless. But in this particular moment of cultural reckoning, it gets at a crucial nuance that seems to have long been missing from the conversation around sexual harassment and assault: that consent isn't always black and white.

Sometimes "yes" means "no," simply because it is easier to go through with it than explain our way out of the situation. Sometimes "no" means "yes," because you actually do want to do it, but you know you're not supposed to lest you be labeled a slut. And if you're a man, that "no" often means "just try harder" — because, you know, persuasion is part of the game.

"A lot of what we as young men learn as seduction is really more like preparatory sexual assault training," the sociologist Harry Brod, a longtime lecturer on the topic of consent, once told me. (Or as a 37-year-old male friend observed: "In a man's mind, 'no' is always negotiable.")

In the 1970s and '80s, when Take Back the Night rallies began cropping up on college campuses, a new antirape slogan emerged: "No means no." Four decades later, that mantra has been all but replaced by a newer version of the consent standard, this one focused on the word "yes," or what's known as the "affirmative consent" model.

As the thinking goes, body language in sexual scenarios can at times be an unreliable factor. So the communication aspect — clearly saying "yes" — is crucial. The default then is no.

Which seems to make a lot of sense, given the fact that, in heterosexual relationships, anyway, men and women have wildly different understandings of consent. In one study, 61 percent of men said they rely on nonverbal cues to indicate whether a partner consents, while only 10 percent of women said they actually give consent via body language.

But what about when "yes" isn't really an enthusiastic affirmative — or an affirmative at all?

The reality is that no matter how many sexual harassment training programs we enroll in, or how much activists extol the virtues of consent, we are missing something deeper: Our idea of what we want — of our own desire — is linked to what we think we're supposed to want, with what society tells us we should want. And most of what society tells us — when it comes to women and sex, anyway — is wrapped in dangerously outdated gender norms.

"Women have been taught, by every cultural force imaginable, that we must be 'nice' and 'quiet' and 'polite.' That we must protect others' feelings before our own. That we are there for others' pleasure," said Rachel Simmons, the author of a number of books on girls, including a new one, "Enough as She Is."

Indeed, women and men learn early that playing hard to get is what's appealing, and part of that chase is saying "no" — and then ultimately relenting.

As Peggy Orenstein, the author of "Girls & Sex," puts it, despite educational gains, despite professional ambition, despite all of it, young women still learn that "our bodies exist for male sexual pleasure, that our 'power' is in attracting male desire." Which can make even seemingly straightforward ideas about sex — such as, you know, whether we want to engage in it or not — feel utterly complex.

Consider the drinking analogy: Most of us understand, or at least we should, that a blackout drunk person cannot consent to sex. On some campuses, that inability to consent applies even if someone has had just a sip or two. But what about a woman who doesn't feel that she can speak up because of cultural expectations? Should that woman be considered unable to consent, too?

In The New Yorker story, the author describes a moment in which the main character almost floats above her body — watching herself perform the sex act almost as if she's a third party. That's a real phenomenon with a name, "spectatoring," and it's more common among girls and women who see their role in sexual encounters as being "desirable" rather than assertive, Ms. Orenstein says.

Like the character, many women have said "yes" to what is happening. Like the character, many of them are thinking to themselves, "This is the worst life decision I have ever made!"

In some respects, it's as if they're in the nosebleed sections of their own sex lives. What will it take for them to come back down?

JESSICA BENNETT is the gender editor of The New York Times and the author of "Feminist Fight Club."

Sex Ed Lesson: 'Yes Means Yes,' but It's Tricky

BY JENNIFER MEDINA | OCT. 14, 2015

SAN FRANCISCO — The classroom of 10th graders had already learned about sexually transmitted diseases and various types of birth control. On this day, the teenagers gathered around tables to discuss another topic: how and why to make sure each step in a sexual encounter is met with consent.

Consent from the person you are kissing — or more — is not merely silence or a lack of protest, Shafia Zaloom, a health educator at the Urban School of San Francisco, told the students. They listened raptly, but several did not disguise how puzzled they felt.

"What does that mean — you have to say 'yes' every 10 minutes?" asked Aidan Ryan, 16, who sat near the front of the room.

"Pretty much," Ms. Zaloom answered. "It's not a timing thing, but whoever initiates things to another level has to ask."

The "no means no" mantra of a generation ago is being eclipsed by "yes means yes" as more young people all over the country are told that they must have explicit permission from the object of their desire before they engage in any touching, kissing or other sexual activity. With Gov. Jerry Brown's signature on a bill this month, California became the first state to require that all high school health education classes give lessons on affirmative consent, which includes explaining that someone who is drunk or asleep cannot grant consent.

Last year, California led the way in requiring colleges to use affirmative consent as the standard in campus disciplinary decisions, defining how and when people agree to have sex. More than a dozen legislatures in other states, including Maryland, Michigan and Utah, are considering similar legislation for colleges. One goal is to improve the way colleges and universities deal with accusations of rape and sexual assault and another is to reduce the number of young people who feel pressured into unwanted sexual conduct.

Critics say the lawmakers and advocates of affirmative consent are trying to draw a sharp line in what is essentially a gray zone, particularly for children and young adults who are grappling with their first feelings of romantic attraction. In he-said, she-said sexual assault cases, critics of affirmative consent say the policy puts an unfair burden of proof on the accused.

"There's really no clear standard yet — what we have is a lot of ambiguity on how these standards really work in the court of law," said John F. Banzhaf III, a professor at George Washington University Law School. "The standard is not logical — nobody really works that way. The problem with teaching this to high school students is that you are only going to sow more confusion. They are getting mixed messages depending where they go afterward."

NOAH BERGER FOR THE NEW YORK TIMES

Juniors and seniors at the Urban School of San Francisco at a forum on affirmative consent.

But Ms. Zaloom, who has taught high school students about sex for two decades, said she was grateful for the new standard, even as she acknowledged the students' unease.

"What's really important to know is that sex is not always super smooth," she told her 10th graders. "It can be awkward, and that's actually normal and shows things are O.K."

The students did not seem convinced. They sat in groups to brainstorm ways to ask for affirmative consent. They crossed off a list of options: "Can I touch you there?" Too clinical. "Do you want to do this?" Too tentative. "Do you like that?" Not direct enough.

"They're all really awkward and bizarre," one girl said.

"Did you come up with any on your own?" Ms. Zaloom asked.

One boy offered up two words: "You good?"

That drew nearly unanimous nods of approval.

Under the new law, high school students in California must be educated about the concept of affirmative consent — but they are not actually being held to that standard. So a high school student on trial on rape charges would not have to prove that he or she obtained oral assent from the accuser. That was the case with a senior at the elite St. Paul's School in New Hampshire this year who was accused of raping a freshman. The senior was acquitted of aggravated sexual assault but found guilty of statutory rape — sex with a minor.

As for college students, the law passed last year in California does not change the way sexual assault cases are prosecuted in criminal courts, only in the way they are handled by colleges, which are permitted to use affirmative consent as a standard.

Last year, Corey Mock, a student at the University of Tennessee-Chattanooga, was expelled after officials there found him guilty of sexual misconduct because he could not prove he had obtained verbal consent from a woman who accused him of sexual assault. But a Davidson County Chancery Court judge ruled in August that the university had "improperly shifted the burden of proof and imposed an untenable standard upon Mr. Mock to disprove the accusation."

The judge called the university's ruling "arbitrary and capricious."

In another case, a former student at Clark University in Worcester, Mass., who was evicted from his dormitory room after a student accused him of rape, filed a lawsuit in federal court in August against the university and several administrators. The former student, identified in court records as John Doe, argued that he had been denied the rights promised in the student handbook and that the adjudicators of his case had ignored text messages that supported his view of the encounter.

Kevin de León, the California State Senate speaker pro tempore and lead sponsor of the high school legislation, said the new law was as much about changing the culture as it was about changing the law.

"Sexual violence has always thrived in the gray areas of the law," Mr. de León said. "What we want to create is a standard of behavior, a paradigm shift as much as a legal shift. We're no longer talking about the old paradigm of the victim being blamed for their own behavior."

But among teenagers, who are only beginning to experiment with their sexuality and have hazy ideas of their own boundaries, the talk tends to be about "hooking up" and what the new rules are. "Kids are still establishing patterns of behavior, and they have a lot of specific concrete questions," said Ms. Zaloom, who has written a curriculum for affirmative consent programs that is being used throughout the country.

Students will ask, "Can I have sex when we are both drunk?" she said. "I get this one a lot: If I hook up with a girl and the next day she decides she didn't want to do it, then what do I do?"

Ms. Zaloom will typically use such questions as a way to begin talking about the benefits of sexual partners' knowing each other. But sometimes, there are no straightforward answers, she said. "We're trying to show them very explicitly that sex has to include a dialogue," she added, "that they have to talk about it each step of the way."

One 10th-grade girl asked about approaching someone about a casual encounter. "What if it's just a one-time thing?"

"You have to be prepared to say 'no' and hear 'no,' " Ms. Zaloom said.

Another girl chimed in, "If you don't care about a person too much, you might not be inclined to listen."

Ms. Zaloom suggested making clear plans with friends ahead of time, like making pacts to leave parties together. And she urged them to have conversations with potential sexual partners "before you get swept up in the moment."

"How do we even start a conversation like that?" one boy wondered.

"Practice," Ms. Zaloom answered.

Eric Schneiderman, Consent and Domestic Violence

BY NIRAJ CHOKSHI | MAY 8, 2018

WHEN FOUR WOMEN accused Eric T. Schneiderman, the New York attorney general, of physical assault this week, he suggested that they were describing consensual sexual encounters.

The allegations against him were new. That defense was not.

Those accused of committing violence against their partners often seek to dismiss those claims, sometimes by arguing that the partners were willing participants in sexual role playing or "rough sex."

Here's a look at the legal and other issues raised by such claims.

'I HAVE ENGAGED IN ROLE-PLAYING'

In a written statement to The New Yorker, included in the article revealing the choking and slapping allegations against him, Mr. Schneiderman denied committing any assault.

"In the privacy of intimate relationships, I have engaged in role-playing and other consensual sexual activity," he wrote. "I have not assaulted anyone. I have never engaged in nonconsensual sex, which is a line I would not cross."

Many men before him have said the same when confronted by such accusations.

In 2014, for example, several women accused Jian Ghomeshi, a well-known Canadian musician and former radio host, of biting, punching, choking and smothering.

In response, he described the activities on Facebook as consensual — "a mild form of 'Fifty Shades of Grey,' " he wrote. (He was ultimately acquitted of sexual assault.)

CONSENT, THE DIVIDING LINE

There is a bright line between pain caused by unwanted sexual or domestic violence and pain that can come during some kinds of consensual sexual activity among willing participants.

"If it's not consensual, then it's not 'rough sex.' It's abuse," said Susan Wright, the founder of the National Coalition for Sexual Freedom, an advocacy organization for a diverse range of sexualities and sexual preferences.

Consent should be given early and often, she said. Limits, risks and how to stop sexual activity should be discussed beforehand. And assumptions should never be made.

"I know some people think it's not sexy or spontaneous to actually talk about sex before you have it," she said. "They're absolutely wrong, because it's the best foreplay in the world to talk about the things that turn you on and find out what things turn the other person on."

Even with consent, if sexual activity causes serious harm, it crosses the line to assault, she said.

A DEFENSE ALSO USED IN KILLINGS

In seeking to explain away their crimes, violent perpetrators have long claimed that victims "asked for it."

But the "rough sex defense" gained notoriety under that name after being used in a high-profile trial in New York in the 1980s.

The trial revolved around the death by strangling of Jennifer Dawn Levin in the summer of 1986.

The night before a bicyclist found her body behind the Metropolitan Museum of Art, Ms. Levin had met up with Robert E. Chambers Jr. at Dorrian's Red Hand, a bar on the Upper East Side. The pair left the bar together at about 4:30 a.m. before walking to Central Park.

Mr. Chambers was immediately suspected in her death and soon became known in the tabloid newspapers of the day as the "Preppy Killer." Until pleading guilty to manslaughter in 1988, he had long insisted that the death was an accident: He said that he had suffocated Ms. Levin by mistake after she hurt him during consensual sex.

What shocked many French people most of all was not the encounter itself, but that there was a legal possibility of labeling it anything other than rape. If legal norms reflect a society's mores, what does this say about France? Petitions started circulating, and politicians would soon echo them: The law must change.

Most European countries have, over the past two decades, set age limits under which a minor simply cannot consent. In Belgium, any sexual intercourse with a child below the age of 14 is rape, punishable up to 20 years, or up to 30 years for victims under 10. In Britain, the age of consent is 16, but specific legal protection exists for children under 13: They cannot legally give their consent to any form of sexual activity. There is a maximum sentence of life imprisonment for "rape, assault by penetration, and causing or inciting a child to engage in sexual activity."

But in France, as long as "violence, coercion, threat or surprise" is not proven, sexual intercourse with a minor — even one under 15 — is considered an "atteinte sexuelle," which is an infraction and not a crime. The trial takes place in a "tribunal correctionnel," which handles infractions, and not at a "cour d'assises," which is for the most serious crimes like murder or rape.

In 2005, the Cour de Cassation, France's highest criminal court, stipulated that coercion is presumed for children at a "very young age." That's an outrageously blurry formulation that in practice has largely been applied to children under 6. This leaves children above 6 potentially considered not raped when violence cannot be established. It also allows the state of paralyzed shock experienced by many victims — and all the more so children — to equal consent.

In 2010, a new law introduced the question of age difference between the victim and the perpetrator from which "moral coercion" could result, expanding the notion of force beyond physical violence. But once again, the difference in age was not precisely qualified. In February 2015, the Constitutional Council reasserted that French law "does not set an age of discernment in regards to sexual relations: It is for the courts to determine whether the minor was capable of consenting to the sexual relationship in question."

France doesn't exactly have a sterling record when it comes to labeling sexual criminality. It took two centuries for sexual crimes against children to be considered so by the law. The penal code of 1810, established by Napoleon, did not say much about sexual behavior, "as if sexuality were not to fall under the law," the philosopher Michel Foucault said in 1978. He deplored the growing "weight" of the laws "controlling" sexuality during the 19th and 20th century.

Foucault was writing a year after the cream of the French intelligentsia published an open letter in Le Monde defending three men charged with having sexual relations with children under the age of 15. The list of signatories included Jean-Paul Sartre, Simone de Beauvoir, Gilles Deleuze, Roland Barthes, Philippe Sollers, André Glucksmann and Louis Aragon. "We consider that there is an incongruity," the letter read, "between the outdated nature of the law and the everyday reality of a society which tends to recognize the existence of a sexual life in children and adolescents (if a 13-year-old girl has the right to be on the pill, what is it for?)."

Interdiction, the thinking went, belonged to the old moral order, and it was considered an honor to children to acknowledge that they had desires.

Fortunately, the mainstream culture has turned away from this pedophile-chic ethos. But if France has continued to be reluctant to define a firm age of consent, it probably has to do with the lingering vestiges of idealized sexual freedom.

And linger it does. When the Roman Polanski case resurfaced in 2009, I remember an outraged Alain Finkielkraut, one of the most visible public intellectuals in France, saying on the radio that Mr. Polanski's 13-year-old victim, Samantha Geimer (nee Gailey), "wasn't a little girl" because she had agreed to be photographed topless, expressing the all too common belief (and likely hope) that girls and boys can indeed be sexual at a young age.

I grew up in Paris, a very free little girl playing in the streets and riding the Metro. By the time I was 15, I had been exposed to more flashers than I care to remember, a few "frotteurs" (men who take advantage of the crowded trains to rub up against their prey), and one man who followed me into my building to have a conversation about my sexual habits when I was about 8. When I was only dreaming about boys my age, I already was very familiar with the chilling effect of adults inserting themselves into my intimate life.

This was how city kids grew up in the aftermath of sexual "liberation": navigating these uncomfortable interactions, unaware we maybe were escaping something worse.

Today, I can't look through the window into a classroom other than my daughter's without being called to order by the headmistress. Still, what horrifies us as a society and seems to belong to common sense — that every instance of sexual intercourse with a child is, by definition, violent — has been left by the law to be examined case by case. The assault in Montmagny must serve as a moral wake-up call for France.

VALENTINE FAURE is writing a book about the Jacqueline Sauvage case.

Who Is the Victim in the Anna Stubblefield Case?

OPINION | BY JEFF MCMAHAN AND PETER SINGER | APRIL 3, 2017

IN OCTOBER 2015, a New Jersey jury convicted Anna Stubblefield, a former professor of ethics at Rutgers University, on two counts of aggravated sexual assault on a 29-year-old man with severe cerebral palsy, known in the court records as D.J. The prosecution claimed that D.J. is sufficiently intellectually disabled to be incapable of consenting to sex and then alleged that Stubblefield had exploited and raped him.

Many of those in the community of advocates for people with disabilities have a different view. Stubblefield has spent much of her career championing the rights of people with disabilities. D.J. was for most of his life regarded as incapable of communication. He continues to be regarded in this way by many. In response to a request from D.J.'s brother, Stubblefield began using a controversial method called facilitated communication that she believes enabled D.J. to express himself. Over a two-year period in which she believes she communicated with him often and deeply, she came to love him and to believe that he loved her and indicated his wish to have sex with her.

Superior Court Judge Siobhan Teare did not allow the defense to present to the jury any evidence of D.J.'s ability to communicate, and decided to exclude all testimony from the defense, apart from that by Stubblefield herself, that in any way related to facilitated communication. In the absence of evidence supporting the defense's contention, the jury convicted Stubblefield. Judge Teare sentenced her to 12 years in prison, with more than 10 of those years to be served without the possibility of parole. Stubblefield is now in prison. She has appealed her conviction, and the appeal will be argued on Tuesday. The court will then have 90 days to hand down its decision.

We are professors of philosophy who have taught in New Jersey, one of us at Rutgers (though not at the same campus as Stubblefield), the other at Princeton. We have met Stubblefield only once, nearly a decade ago, at a conference on cognitive disability and moral philosophy. We were invited to this conference, which was organized by philosophers who are advocates for the cognitively disabled, as devil's advocates whose challenges to common views about the moral status of profoundly cognitively impaired human beings and the permissibility of ending the lives of some newborn infants with severe disabilities were strongly criticized, not least by Stubblefield herself. In her philosophical work she has been and remains our determined adversary. We have no reason to be biased in her favor and our concern with this case is entirely disinterested.

After studying the evidence advanced by Stubblefield's attorney in support of her appeal, we are astonished by Judge Teare's refusal to admit evidence that could have exonerated Stubblefield, while admitting contrary evidence from the prosecution. We also believe that, even if every factual claim made by the prosecution were true, a sentence of 12 years in prison would be utterly disproportionate to the nature of the crime.

In facilitated communication, the facilitator supports the arm or hand of a disabled person while that person touches a keyboard to spell out words. The method is claimed by some to be particularly useful for people who, like D.J., are unable to speak and have great difficulty in controlling their limbs. But most studies have failed to show the method's effectiveness, and some have shown that facilitators can, without intending to deceive anyone, come to believe that they are enabling a disabled person to communicate when in fact they are the ones who are writing the sentences. The studies cannot, however, prove that Stubblefield was misled in this way, and independent evidence suggests that D.J. is literate and able to communicate.

Sheronda Jones, an undergraduate at Rutgers at the time, volunteered to assist D.J. by using facilitated communication so that he could write papers for an English class he was auditing at Rutgers. Before the trial, Jones had told a detective in the Essex County Prosecutor's

Office: "He pretty much read the books. I didn't know any information about the book. I made sure never to read any of the information. I can't tell you what he read. And he typed out the information." Jones did not attend the class D.J. took. If she did not read the material on which his work was based, how could she have produced writings that respond to that material?

The defense wanted to put Jones on the witness stand. Judge Teare refused, and the jury knew nothing of her interview with the detective.

Rosemary Crossley, the defense's expert on communicating with people with physical disabilities, assessed D.J.'s ability to communicate, spending 12 hours with him over three days, and found that he "wanted to communicate and was able to communicate, given appropriate strategies." Her assessment was filmed by cameras in two positions. It was not based on facilitated communication but on methods that could have been viewed and judged by the jurors, such as requiring D.J. to touch, unaided, a "yes" or "no" button on a communication device and to answer multiple-choice questions, most of which he had to read for himself. Under these conditions, D.J. correctly answered 43 of 45 factual questions. The judge refused to allow Crossley to testify about her assessment, claiming that Crossley improperly assisted D.J. during the evaluation. The judge also did not allow the members of the jury to see the videos, which would have enabled them to judge for themselves whether Crossley had influenced the outcome.

She did, however, permit the prosecution to display D.J. to the jury for a few moments in his mute and spastic condition. It is well established in the psychological literature that people tend to infer cognitive disability from severe physical disability, especially when the disabled individual is unable to speak. There is no reason to suppose that the members of the jury were immune to this tendency. Yet fewer than 50 percent of those with cerebral palsy have any degree of cognitive impairment. In an amicus brief, intended to be heard in conjunction with Stubblefield's appeal, the American Civil Liberties Union, joined by various disability rights organizations, said that in exhibiting D.J. to the jury in this manner, the court had failed to protect his rights. The appellate court, however, has refused to consider the A.C.L.U.'s brief.

Judge Teare's exclusion of Jones's and Crossley's testimonies means that the jury's verdict was given in ignorance of vital evidence. It also suggests the possibility that D.J. himself is now in a situation akin to "locked-in syndrome," finding himself suddenly deprived of any means of communication after two years of being able to express his thoughts through Stubblefield and Jones. To determine whether this is true, his ability to communicate via facilitated communication should be established by independent testing. This should be done for his sake and for Stubblefield's.

Suppose, however, that all these doubts about Stubblefield's conviction are mistaken. Even on that assumption, a sentence of 12 years in prison is excessive both in itself and in comparison with other recent punishments. It is, for example, in striking contrast to the penalty given to Brock Turner, the former Stanford student who is now free after serving only three months of a six-month sentence for raping an unconscious woman. The contrast does not indicate whether Turner's sentence was too lenient, or Stubblefield's too harsh. It does, however, suggest that we should think carefully about what considerations are relevant to sentencing for sex crimes. In determining how severe a sentence is appropriate for a sex crime, it seems obvious that the beliefs and intentions of the perpetrator and the harm done to the victim are among the most important considerations.

Judge Teare described Stubblefield as "the perfect example of a predator preying on her prey" and gave her a sentence that would be fitting for a predatory rapist. Yet no one would or could ever have known that Stubblefield and D.J. had had sexual relations if she had not conveyed to his mother and brother what she believed to be his message to them, via facilitated communication that she conducted in their presence, that he and she were in love and had consummated their relationship. This is the action not of a sexual predator but of an honest and honorable woman in love. Even if she is mistaken in her beliefs about his intelligence and ability to communicate, it is undeniable that these beliefs are sincere and that she was neither reckless nor negligent in forming them. This ought to have been a mitigating, if not wholly exculpating, consideration in the sentencing.

The severity of the judge's sentence might be justifiable if Stubblefield's having sex with D.J. not only was culpable but also both wronged him and harmed him. Yet both of the latter assumptions are questionable.

A central issue in the trial was whether D.J. is profoundly cognitively impaired, as the prosecution contended and the court seemed to accept, or is competent cognitively but unable to communicate his thoughts without highly skilled assistance, as the defense contended. If we assume that he is profoundly cognitively impaired, we should concede that he cannot understand the normal significance of sexual relations between persons or the meaning and significance of sexual violation. These are, after all, difficult to articulate even for persons of normal cognitive capacity. In that case, he is incapable of giving or withholding informed consent to sexual relations; indeed, he may lack the concept of consent altogether.

This does not exclude the possibility that he was wronged by Stubblefield, but it makes it less clear what the nature of the wrong might be. It seems reasonable to assume that the experience was pleasurable to him; for even if he is cognitively impaired, he was capable of struggling to resist, and, for reasons we will note shortly, it is implausible to suppose that Stubblefield forcibly subdued him. On the assumption that he is profoundly cognitively impaired, therefore, it seems that if Stubblefield wronged or harmed him, it must have been in a way that he is incapable of understanding and that affected his experience only pleasurably.

If, by contrast, we assume that he has normal cognitive capacities, certain uncontested facts make it difficult to believe that he was forced to have sex against his will — for example, that he cooperated in the process of revealing to his family that he and Stubblefield had had sexual relations. On the assumption that he has normal cognitive abilities, he would surely have found a way to express his hostility to Stubblefield on that occasion or subsequently. Evidence of such hostility would have strengthened the prosecution's case. The prosecution, however, offered no evidence that D.J. had ever shown hostility to Stubblefield.

This is hard to reconcile with the assumption that D.J. has normal cognitive capacities and had been forcibly subjected to sexual abuse by Stubblefield.

For someone to spend 12 years in prison for a sexual act that took place in the context of a long-term, caring relationship that was motivated by love — at least on Stubblefield's part — and about which there is no evidence that it caused any harm is, in our view, outrageous.

In October 2016, it was announced that D.J.'s family, which had filed a civil suit against Stubblefield, had been awarded $4 million by another New Jersey court — $2 million in compensatory damages and $2 million in punitive damages. The press report quotes the family's attorney as saying that "my clients are victims of a horrible predator," to which he added the gloating comment that "she's got 12 years to think about it."

But just as there is little reason to suppose that Stubblefield harmed D.J., so it is difficult to see what harm she inflicted on his family members. If anything, she tried to help them by working to communicate with D.J. for two years without asking for or receiving any fee. She has now endured a harrowing trial, is separated from her teenage daughter and is facing 12 years in prison. Despite the complexities of the incident and the trial, we believe that Stubblefield herself is a victim of grievous and unjust harms.

JEFF MCMAHAN, formerly a professor of philosophy at Rutgers University, is a professor of moral philosophy at the University of Oxford. **PETER SINGER** is a professor of bioethics at Princeton University and laureate professor at the University of Melbourne.

CHAPTER 2

Consent on Campus

Universities have found themselves at the center of the
debate over sexual consent. Campuses have reeled from
a series of prominent sexual assault cases and have struggled to identify solutions to the problem. The articles in
this section demonstrate how young people and academic
institutions negotiate the issue of sexual consent. They
also illustrate the culture of sexual violence that has grown
on university campuses and the very real consequences
for its victims.

Campus Sex . . . With a Syllabus

BY JESSICA BENNETT | JAN. 9, 2016

HARTFORD — "Where did I learn about sexual consent?"

Jonathan Kalin was standing before an auditorium of Trinity College freshmen, pressing play on a clip from the movie "Superbad."

The 2007 film, you may recall, tells the story of two schlubby high
school friends on a quest to lose their virginity before college. In
this particular scene, the main characters, played by Jonah Hill and
Michael Cera, are standing in the middle of a soccer scrimmage dis-
secting whether or not Mr. Hill's romantic interest wants to hook up
with him. The evidence, in this case, is booze: She had asked him to
help her buy some for her party.

Mr. Hill relays a familiar scenario to his friend: Girl gets drunk at
party; girl has sex with guy; the next morning, girl regrets what happened. He pauses, excitedly. "We could be that mistake!"

Jonathan Kalin, the founder of the organization Party With Consent, talks to freshmen at Trinity College in Hartford.

The students in the room laughed, albeit hesitantly. This was a lecture about consent, after all.

"So what did we just learn about sexual consent from Michael Cera and Jonah Hill?" Mr. Kalin asked.

"There wasn't any, really," a young man in the front called out.

"Exactly," Mr. Kalin said. "It's not just that it's O.K. to get drunk and have sex with them, it's that it's actually cool."

Mr. Kalin is the 24-year-old founder of a group called Party With Consent — a slogan displayed in neon behind him (and on T-shirts he would later hand out). On this Saturday, he had traveled from Providence, R.I., where he worked at the Swearer Center for Public Service at Brown University, to Hartford to speak to Trinity students about the importance of understanding what has become a campus buzzword of late: consent.

The lecture, which he would give four times on this day, to four different groups of students, was part of a sexual assault curriculum that

Trinity College freshmen were required to complete (and had their attendance recorded to ensure it).

It was followed, later that night, by an actual "party with consent" — an all-ages event with bands, an open bar and bowls of colorful condoms that read, "Did you ask consent?" Trinity was one of the half-dozen campuses Mr. Kalin had visited since the school year began.

"In my experience, when you ask men on college campuses where they learned about consent, they sort of look at you blankly and say, 'What do you mean?' " Mr. Kalin said to a reporter. "This is meant to be like a pre-intro intro course. Hopefully it's a gateway to a larger conversation."

In the movies (that are not "Superbad"), sexual consent goes something like this: the lights dim, the mood swells, two people silently move toward each other at the same exact time, knowing what the other wants without speaking a word. Clothes come off seamlessly; lovemaking ensues. Consent is implied, not spoken.

But in real life — and, ever more frequently, on college campuses — what constitutes consent is wildly more complicated. Sometimes one person initiates; other times it's both; still other times it's hard to tell. Sometimes one party wants to engage in part of the sex act but not all of it; other times a person may consent to doing one thing at one moment, only to withdraw that consent as the thing actually begins to happen.

In some cases one party reads a signal — a physical cue, a look, a text message, something else — to mean one thing, while the other intended it to mean something entirely different.

No, most rape is not the result of a misunderstanding. To the contrary, one-fourth to two-thirds of rapists are serial attackers, studies show. And yet how we understand consent has been at the core of a number of recent rape cases, and it is a focus of a growing field of study. When it comes to young people today, and college, and hooking up, and drinking, and rape culture, and consent, there's enough confusion that the services of people like Mr. Kalin are in high demand.

The statistics by this point are familiar: More than one in five college women will become victims of sexual assault, most of them by somebody they know, with very few coming forward to report the crimes. In the vast majority of these cases (80 percent, according to a 2009 study), alcohol is involved, for both women and men.

More surprising, perhaps, is that the way men and women understand consent is in almost direct opposition to each other: One study found that 61 percent of men say they rely on nonverbal cues — body language — to indicate if a woman is consenting to a sexual act, while only 10 percent of women say they actually give consent via body language (most say they wait to be asked).

"People often ask, 'Why teach consent?' " said the sociologist Harry Brod, a professor at the University of Northern Iowa and a longtime lecturer on the topic of consent. His answer: "Because we often have entirely different understandings of what it means."

Mr. Kalin's own lecture grew out of that realization, as part of a group he was involved in as an undergraduate at Colby College, where he was captain of the basketball team, called Male Athletes Against Violence. At the time, he had noticed a tasteless slogan cropping up on T-shirts on and around campus. It read, "Party With Sluts." Mr. Kalin decided to turn the slogan on its head.

He's no longer a rare voice, as college campuses across the country, responding to increased scrutiny, incorporate consent education programs into their curriculums.

A number of campuses have adopted a program called "Consent Is Sexy," a poster campaign and workshop series developed by a psychologist and a former campus minister that can be tailored to individual campuses. There is a traveling assault education improv show called "Sex Signals," while new students at Columbia must complete a course in "sexual respect." During the fall orientation at the University of California, Irvine, a video featuring student actors explained that "consent is knowing your partner wants you as much as you want them."

The rise of these programs lies in evolving federal guidelines about how universities must handle response to, and prevention of, sexual assault on campus. NotAlone.gov, the government website devoted to Title IX compliance, recommends that universities define consent for students, including language to indicate that, among other things, consent cannot be granted by somebody who is incapacitated; that past consent does not imply future consent; and that consent can be withdrawn at any time.

Trinity is among the estimated 1,500 colleges and universities that, along with state systems in California and New York, have adopted what is known as the "affirmative consent" standard, which requires students to consent with a clear indication of "yes" — sometimes every step of the way — in turn making the default response (or no response at all) "no."

It is a shift from the "no means no" mantra of a generation ago, the idea being that having to give, or ask for, a clear "yes" will help eliminate ambiguity.

And yet there is a learning curve.

Campuses like Trinity's have thick handbooks full of sexual assault resources, filled with pages upon pages of legal definitions and situational scenarios. But that doesn't mean that students necessarily understand the new policies. Yes, "consent" is now emblazoned on T-shirts and posters — it was the subject of a recent public service initiative at Columbia, "Consent is BAE," that was criticized by students — but even that does not ensure that students can define it.

"I think it's when two people agree to have sex, yeah?" a young woman, a junior at the Fashion Institute of Technology, said when approached on a recent day in Manhattan and asked if she could define "affirmative consent."

"Isn't that when only yes means yes? But not really?" said another woman, a dance and fashion major at N.Y.U.

"I know what consent is; is this different?" said a young man, a sports management major, also at N.Y.U.

And there is a whole new vocabulary to memorize, with terms like "enthusiastic consent," "implied consent," "spectrum of consent," "reluctant permission," "coercion" and "unintentional rape." Even "yes means yes," the slogan of the anti-rape movement is sort of confusing.

"It should be 'Only yes means yes,' " said Dr. Brod, the sociologist. (And if you still can't tell, then ask.)

The questions from students are seemingly endless: Can consent only be given verbally, or can it be indicated by body language (and if so, how can I be sure it "counts")? What's the difference between "affirmative," "enthusiastic" and "effective consent," and why do all of these terms vary by campus (and sometimes even within them)? How does a person gauge or indicate interest, or demonstrate consent, without having to awkwardly ask, "Is this O.K.?" a thousand times over again (or is this simply the new norm)?

Even in the best situations, it can take some getting used to.

Seated with a group of students in the women's center after Mr. Kalin's talk, Caroline Howell, a sophomore at Trinity, described a hookup scenario with a guy who — every step of the way — asked for her permission.

"As much as I was like, 'This is awesome,' I was like: 'This is weird. This is awkward,' " she said. "And then I was like, 'Wait, we went through that whole thing and I didn't ask a single question — shouldn't I be asking too?' "

Then there is the drinking issue. Campus policies are clear about the inability of a person to consent if she or he is drunk (or, in other words, if Jonah Hill acted out his wish, he could be considered a rapist). But what if a student has just one beer — or even just a sip?

"I think one of the biggest misconceptions about consent is around alcohol consumption," said Emily Kaufman, a sophomore at Trinity.

"Yes," another young woman said. "Like, if you have one sip of alcohol you can't consent."

"And girls too," Ms. Kaufman added. "They think, 'If I drink at all, I can't have sex that night?' "

Trinity's definition states that if a person is "mentally or physically incapacitated or impaired so that such person cannot understand the fact, nature or extent of the situation, there is no consent." But what does that really mean?

"These things are very tidy on paper, but in the private sphere, with two people going into a room, bringing with them expectations and assumptions, very often they are not on the same page," said Jason Laker, a professor at San Jose State University, who, with a colleague, Erica Boas, created a project called Consent Stories, which aims to document how students communicate consent.

"There's a big gap between the laws and policies that stipulate consent, and people's understanding of it," Dr. Laker said.

There is also seemingly nobody keeping track of how it's being taught: no governing body to review these programs; no standardized definition of consent; nor much research into types of prevention strategies that work. It's not dissimilar, said Senator Kirsten Gillibrand, a Democrat of New York, to how campuses have handled their response to cases of sexual assault: with little uniformity. (Senator Gillibrand is the co-sponsor of a bill that would create a standard for those response procedures, including bringing in credentialed experts.)

"I think a certain amount of chaos is expected when you're going through social change," said Jaclyn Friedman, a longtime sex educator and the co-editor of a book called "Yes Means Yes!" "But I also think there's still a lot of confusion."

Mr. Kalin hopes he can try to close the gap, or at least make students think about the culture that surrounds it. At Trinity, he peppered his talks with pop culture details and references to LeBron James in an effort to speak to students in "their language." He also discussed "sexist foundations," "notions of masculinity," "social constructs of gender," "social hierarchies" — gender studies terminology to which many in his audience appeared to stare blankly.

He shared some of his most vulnerable stories: the death of his father in an auto accident, when he was 12, and how it affected his perceptions of manhood; finding out in college that a woman he knew had been sexually assaulted (and assuming that that type of crime could never happen on his campus).

But if his message at times gets lost in the nuance, others are lost in the simplicity.

At N.Y.U., one part of the sexual misconduct training freshmen are required to attend takes the form of a musical. "I mean, N.Y.U. is a great school, it has a great drama program, but it's still a musical about consent," said Meghan Racklin, a senior. Ms. Racklin is a founder of a photography initiative called #BetterSexTalk, which asks students to answer the question, "If you could give one piece of advice to a younger sibling about sex, what would it be?" ("A crash-course in sexual respect during college orientation," the group's website reads, "will never atone for years of inadequate sex ed.")

Some schools use the language of traffic lights (if you're in the yellow, you must get to red or green), while others show a popular YouTube video that compares consent to tea ("If you say 'Hey, would you like a cup of tea?' and they're like, 'Uh, you know, I'm not really sure,' then you can make them a cup of tea, or not, but be aware they might not drink it," the video explains.)

In one workshop in Manhattan, led by Dr. Brod, an audience member told a story of a sex educator in Philadelphia who uses a pizza analogy to explain consent. ("When people decide to eat pizza, there's a discussion about toppings," the man said.) Sports analogies are useful. So is candy. ("If I know Jessica likes candy, and I've shared it with her in the past, is it O.K. for her to take my bag of candy without my consent, even if I'm putting it in front of her face?")

Back at Trinity, Abdul Staten, the training and program coordinator at the Women & Gender Resource Action Center, which hosted Mr. Kalin, described using a roller-coaster analogy: If you're trying to convince a friend to go on a roller-coaster ride with you, but they don't want to, what are you going to do to try to convince them?

"The students respond with things like, 'I'd bribe her,' 'I'd give her pretzels,' 'I'd offer to hold her hand,' " Mr. Staten said. "They yell out all these things that are somewhat coercive, and then I say: 'So let's say you're in a dating situation and someone says all these things to you, and you go along with it. Are you giving consent?'

"I get that that's a really surface way of looking at it," he continued, "but with a lot of survivors, it's not about being held down. It's like, 'He kept asking, so I finally said yes,' or 'I didn't want to be rude,' or 'He wouldn't leave so I just did so he would.' "

Of course, part of the teaching is all about context. What do you actually say if you want to say stop, or are unsure, or need a minute to think about it? Are there ways to indicate you're into it without having to say yes over and over again?

And what about the larger cultural framework? How do you tackle these concepts in a world where women are empowered to say yes — but taught that they must be coy when they do it? When they've been socialized to think that "yes" means you're a slut, "maybe" means you're a tease, and "no" means you're a prude — or that, from the male perspective, as one friend recently put it, "no is always negotiable"?

"I think that if you're going to teach about consent, you need to also talk about culture," said Jing Qu, a junior at Columbia who has been involved in activism around consent education on campus. "It's the oversexualization of female bodies on TV and in magazines. It's this idea of like: 'Oh does she want it? She won't give me a straight answer.' It's the idea that she's 'asking for it.' It's literally like Justin Bieber saying" — while rolling around half-naked on a bed with a woman in his new video — " 'What do you mean?' " (It's the title of his new song.)

Mr. Kalin, for what it's worth, tries to fit his talk into the bigger context. Back in the auditorium, he asked the Trinity students which nights were the "party nights" on campus.

The room was silent.

"Now tell me: On a party night, before men go out, what do we tell them to do?" he asked.

"What about women?" he said. "What do we tell them to do before a night out?"

The students suddenly became animated.

"Stick together," a woman in the front said.

"Travel in groups," another called out.

"Don't put down your drink." "Dress appropriately."

"Put your keys between your knuckles."

Mr. Kalin nodded. "Does anyone have any idea where I'm going with this?"

What the Weinstein Effect Can Teach Us About Campus Sexual Assault

OPINION | BY VANESSA GRIGORIADIS | NOV. 15, 2017

THE OUTPOURING OF EMOTION over stories of sexual harassment in the workplace has been shocking and inspiring. After Harvey Weinstein's sins were reported by The New York Times and The New Yorker, women (and men) in entertainment and a host of other industries have come forward with sickening tales of their own. The calls for greater accountability — meaning sustainable change beyond companies firing a handful of terrible, famous men — seem genuine.

This moment of clarifying anger is particularly impressive given the recent lack of respect paid to another type of victim, one who dominated the news directly before Mr. Weinstein's fall from grace: the college sexual assault victim. Even as debate about sexual harassment at institutions as disparate as Fox News and Artforum rages on, we have entered a period of backlash regarding student-on-student sexual assault on campus.

About six years ago, colleges began offering better support and justice for victims, pushed in part by a grass-roots movement among students themselves. But in September, pundits across the political spectrum approved when the Education Department rolled back some Obama-era rules that had broadened protections for college sexual assault victims, ostensibly because they robbed accused students of their right to due process in campus courts. Obama's rules were already pro forma at some colleges before his 2011 federal guidance, so I believe the backlash isn't truly about government policy, but discomfort about the change in how students approach the problem of sexual assault today.

The number of students who have come forward publicly with stories of sexual assault has skyrocketed, but the number of students who are willing to report sexual assault to their administrators is still relatively tiny. In 2014, 20.2 million students attended college in the United States, but they reported only about 6,700 sexual assault incidents to their universities compared with 2,200 reports in 2001. The increased visibility of victims in college may seem alarming, but it almost certainly does not reflect a spike in the number of sexual assaults. It reflects a much more positive trend: Like today's actresses, college students are casting off the shame of victimhood to tell their stories.

I witnessed this firsthand as I traveled to four-year residential universities around the country to interview students, administrators and parents about the state of sex on campus. What I heard was exciting in many respects: Young women are becoming more comfortable with asserting their bodily autonomy. Their growing refusal to submit to nonconsensual encounters should count as progress. How this plays out on campus is different from the Weinstein effect in key ways, but the point is, students have been at the forefront of what it means to be more outspoken about misconduct. They also offer us a preview of where the country might be going next.

Campus sexual assault may be a trickier problem for society than workplace harassment of subordinates. When one of the most successful producers in the history of Hollywood uses his lofty position to lure powerless young actresses into hotel rooms to violate them, it's easy to regard him as a monster. There's a different dynamic on college campuses. Despite the clichés about predatory football stars targeting defenseless freshman girls, student-on-student sexual assault often doesn't involve an obvious power differential. It also rarely happens during daytime classes or university-sponsored activities, or in the regulated spaces that might be more analogous to a workplace. Sexual assault happens mostly in students' social lives, at fraternity houses, off-campus apartments and dorms.

The dynamics of sexual immaturity at colleges have also blurred the lines slightly. Students have varying amounts of sex education and were more likely to learn what they know from pornography or other media that perpetuate America's toxic gender norms — the kind that may teach a boy to push an unwilling girl as hard as he can in the bedroom because that's how a real man has sex. Add to that parties, drinking, lack of supervision and an absurd amount of student leisure time on some residential campuses, and you get all sorts of messy situations, particularly of the type involving blacked-out students.

What's more, on campuses today, the definition of sexual assault is broader than elsewhere in the country. The criminal standard for sexual assault varies greatly from state to state, but groping isn't usually much more than a misdemeanor, if that. Yet at many universities, both public and private, students must hew to an extraordinarily high standard of communication to ensure that their sexual conduct is appropriate and consensual. These students must follow some principle of "affirmative consent," which is colloquially called "yes means yes." Reckless abandon in the bedroom doesn't cut it. Students must receive a spoken "yes" or an unmistakable sign of pleasure or consent from a partner to escalate, and proceed with, each stage of a sexual encounter.

"Yes means yes" is a great standard. It could help many men (both in college and out of it) proceed not only with caution but also with compassion for their sexual partners, because they must regard them as individuals with sexual desires rather than merely objects of gratification. But "yes means yes" is still a high bar for students, who as a cohort know very little about sex, let alone how to talk about it. By and large, kids aren't taught the right vocabulary to distinguish between sexual assault and bad sex. This means that a number of accused college men are caught in a time of transition about our understanding of the definition of sexual assault.

On campus, the young college women and men I met were not, by and large, arguing about whether certain acts occurred in the bedroom. Many young men who say they have been falsely accused of sexual assault do not deny that the sex at issue happened in the way their accusers described it. Instead, they argue that their conduct — while perhaps not outstanding and worthy of gold stars — was still acceptable. It's not "yes, you did!" versus "no, I didn't"; it's "yes, it was consensual!" versus "no, it wasn't!"

The solution is not to roll back protections for students, but to be clearer about expectations for them and create more avenues in college (and earlier) to talk about sexual respect and ethics. Because what students complain about — even when it doesn't rise to the level of assault — is often deeply demeaning. While most students I met agreed that a student who snakes a hand under a girl's dress is guilty of assault, some of them argued that a guy who grinds on a classmate on the dance floor without permission is guilty of the same. Both are examples of disrespect, though to me the first is the only one that rises to the level of sexual assault.

As more and more women (and men) come forward about their sexual assaults at the hands of famous individuals or in the workplace, the adult world will have plenty of confusion about "what counts," too. There will be stories where the definition of consent will be in dispute, as on campus, and the risk of a post-Weinstein backlash is just as possible.

The cultural shift around sexual assault is a necessarily messy process, one that will take years to resolve fully, and it involves a lot more than reining in powerful men. We must encourage discussions among one another by carefully broadening our understanding of sexual violence. At the same time, we should educate young people on appropriate behavior rather than cutting them off by focusing on insufficient due process in campus courts.

In the meantime, we should be reassured that there is very much a positive side to this cultural upheaval: Kids in college are starting to talk about sex in a more personal and open way than ever before, and not just as a matter of politics but as a matter of pleasure. They've learned, as one female student put it, that "sex is about me too. I'm supposed to be enjoying this. It's not all about you."

VANESSA GRIGORIADIS, a contributing writer at The New York Times Magazine, is the author of "Blurred Lines: Rethinking Sex, Power, and Consent on Campus."

On the Front Line of Campus Sexual Misconduct

BY KATHERINE ROSMAN | SEPT. 26, 2015

ANN ARBOR, MICH. — Sarah Daniels stood at the front of an auditorium on the University of Michigan campus and looked out at the 120 or so students before her on an unseasonably cool day in late August.

The first day of classes was about two weeks away. But for many of these students, their education had already begun.

"We want people to have sex with people they want to have sex with," Ms. Daniels told the students in their maize-and-blue T-shirts, Birkenstocks and backward baseball caps. "You are the front lines. You can be a role model, step in and say, 'It's not O.K.,' or, 'Be safe!' "

The room erupted in appreciative finger snapping (the new clapping).

The students, a near-even split of men and women and nearly a third of the university's 400 student resident hall advisers, had come to hear Ms. Daniels, the assistant dean of students, give a talk entitled "Sexual Misconduct and Bystander Intervention: What It Is and What to Do About It." It was one of three speeches she would give that day.

In the audience for one of those sessions was Sarah Hong, a senior. Ms. Hong, 20, who grew up in Seoul and Vancouver, British Columbia, is majoring in biopsychology, cognition and neuroscience, with a minor in community action and social change. She is an R.A. in Oxford Housing and has been charged with overseeing 26 mostly first-year students. She is also a member of student organizations that address campus leadership and sexual misconduct.

During her freshman year, Ms. Hong said, a friend told her that she had been sexually assaulted, and counseling the friend was formative. "It was a devastating experience, even for me," she said. Other people "in the community," Ms. Hong said, were not taking her friend's situation seriously. "I was confused by that. No one seemed to care and I didn't know what resources to direct her to. I didn't know how to deal with something so serious."

As a sophomore she decided to become a volunteer for Sapac, short for the university's Sexual Assault Prevention and Awareness Center, committing to a 40-hour training program that prepared her for the role as a confidential student counselor. As an R.A., her obligations are different. If someone discloses information about a possible violation of the school's sexual misconduct policy, she must report it to a resident hall supervisor.

It can be a tough balancing act: being part of the university's staff and still acting as a sensitive friend to a dormitory neighbor.

"My job as an R.A. is to reassure them, to make sure they know of all the resources: that's most important," Ms. Hong said of students who might report sexual misconduct. "People panic, they say, 'Oh, everyone will know about this now!' It's my job to reassure them that they still have control of the situation. It's my job to be a friend and to establish trust."

Helping teenagers make the transition from high schoolers in their parents' homes to college students balancing the freedoms of an unchaperoned social life with the load of academic expectations has always been a big job for R.A.s, most of whom are no older than 21 themselves.

But in recent years, the job has become much more intense. The federal government has laid out new guidelines about universities' responsibilities in investigating, addressing and responding to allegations of student sexual misconduct. These measures have helped open a national conversation about sex and sexual assault on campus, and the role of the university in prevention, awareness and disciplinary measures. At the same time, binge-drinking and drug-taking, which often play a role in campus sex and sexual misconduct, continue to escalate.

Last week, the Association of American Universities released the findings of a sexual misconduct survey that culled data from more than 150,000 undergraduate, graduate and professional students at 27 universities. In it, nearly one in four undergraduate women said they were victims of sexual assault or misconduct. At Harvard College alone, 16 percent of female seniors said that during their time at Harvard they were subjected to "nonconsensual completed or attempted penetration."

During the winter of 2015, the University of Michigan conducted its own study to try to quantify the frequency of sexual assault. The Campus Climate Survey on Sexual Misconduct found 22.5 percent of undergraduate females and 6.8 percent of undergraduate males said they have experienced nonconsensual kissing, touching or penetration. "In most cases, the unwanted sexual penetration occurred primarily after verbal pressure, and under the influence of drugs or alcohol," the study said.

The school has been publicizing the results widely among its faculty and students. Ms. Daniels said: "I work in this field, so I knew the results would be dismaying, but even I was surprised by the numbers. It is sobering, very, very sobering."

Schools like Michigan are offering workshops for new students on how to have discussions about sex, which is admirable even if administrators are somewhat optimistic in believing teenagers and 20-somethings will be comfortable having conversations about a topic that remains, for many adults, difficult to openly address. Complicating the matter is a university climate of political correctness that instills in students a fear of offending others and that hampers open dialogue.

Ms. Hong has helped lead workshops for incoming students that focus on consent. But students come from so many different backgrounds, and with such a spectrum of sexual experience and sexual education, that it can be difficult to know what they understand.

"You can be talking to students about consent and contraception methods and someone will say, 'Oh, at my high school we were just taught not to do it,' " Ms. Hong said. "I am often wondering if students are just sitting there, confused."

Even as R.A.s are encouraged to befriend and offer mentorship to the students on their floors, they are designated "mandatory reporters" of any incident that may violate the school policy on sexual misconduct, which accounts for a range of behavior from rape to sending explicit photographs of someone over the Internet without their consent. Even something as difficult to measure as texting someone more than they may desire can warrant a report.

Megan McDonald, 21, is the resident coordinator for Stockwell Hall, which means she has an overall responsibility for the dorm's 400 students, with direct accountability for about 50. A senior and a public policy major, Ms. McDonald sits down with her agenda at the beginning of the week and tries to carve out 25 hours to address her residents and their needs and another 25 hours for homework and studying. Sometimes, the dedicated R.A. time is spent trying to make friends with the students living in Stockwell, even as she lets them know that she cannot keep confidential anything they tell her related to sexual misconduct.

"It's a hindrance on your social life because you know if a friend confides in you, you can't necessarily keep it a secret," Ms. McDonald said. "It's one of the burdens of having this role."

But she said she believes it's important to put her R.A. job before friendship. "During training, we talk about it and we try to remember, this is somebody's kid, this could be your kid one day," she said.

And it can be hard to shut off the worry that R.A.s almost necessarily feel. Amanda Champagne, 20, is a senior who is applying for master's programs for social work. When she and her friends go to parties, she takes care to be sure that her group leaves with everyone it arrived with and that no one walks home alone. "My friends will make fun of me and say, 'Amanda, you're in R.A. mode.' They call me the mom of the group," she said. "Being an R.A. has enhanced my understanding of the university, so I do feel like I have a heightened awareness, especially about sexual assault."

R.A. gigs at Michigan are hard to come by, with "hundreds" of applicants being turned down, according to a school spokesman. The university's housing department staff chooses candidates based on their academic record and commitment to campus leadership. R.A.s are selected during the fall term of the previous academic year and then are required to take a class on community building. R.A.s are compensated with free room and board, which otherwise costs about $10,000 for the academic year.

"More so than anyone else on campus, you will meet and connect with so many students," Ms. Daniels said.

It was Day 2 of R.A. training and she and a few colleagues were outlining the university's student sexual misconduct policy.

This year, Ms. Daniels made her presentation not only to the R.A.s but also to the school's student-athletes, members of R.O.T.C., the marching band and the leaders of the school's Greek system, among others. "We go after groups that we know have influence on campus," she said in an interview.

While law enforcement agencies oversee their own investigations and prosecutions of reported incidents of sex crimes, the University of Michigan's policy lays out the school's definitions of sexual misconduct and its particular process when an incident has been reported to school officials, including R.A.s.

The R.A.s seem to grapple with the concept of their dual roles as students living among peers in a dorm and university staff with obligations. "What if someone tells you something before you've told them you're a mandatory reporter?" one student asked at the workshop. "Is it like Miranda rights?"

Ms. Daniels answered, "It's important that you tell your residents upfront that you are not confidential," explaining that a student who may have been harmed by an alleged act of sexual misconduct need not participate in an investigation.

During the next 90 minutes, Ms. Daniels and her cohort went over key themes: that an act of retaliation against a complainant who says she or he has been a victim of misconduct is itself a violation of the misconduct policy, that the Internet can be a tool of sexual misconduct, and that "intoxicated" people can consent to sexual contact but those "incapacitated" by excess drugs and alcohol cannot.

A student asked, "How do you determine the difference between intoxication and incapacitation?"

The answer was murky, underscoring how hard it is for adults, let alone college students, to identify clear lines. "Incapacitation is beyond intoxication, when you're unable to make informed judgment, just totally unable," Ms. Daniels said. "It's a case-by-case thing," she said, adding that she wished she could provide more clarity.

Into a world of many acronyms and mnemonic devices, the four Ds of bystander intervention were introduced: direct, distract, delegate and delay. The women leading the session explained the importance of R.A.s learning how to intervene (and teaching their dorm residents to intervene) in potentially harmful situations they may witness.

Different scenarios were posed, with students asking how they might respond. "You are at a party and see a man pulling someone who is obviously intoxicated up the stairs toward an empty room," went one example. The room buzzed as students offered ideas.

One student suggested approaching the man carrying the other person and trying to distract him. "You could say, like, 'Hey, we're in psych class together,' " the student said.

The concept of intervention was not new to many students, and some were moved to share their own experiences.

One said that on a snowy night last year, she and a friend happened to drive by Rick's, a bar that bills itself on Twitter as "The #1 Hook up bar on college campuses!"

They spotted a woman stumbling down the sidewalk with a man. The friends called out to the woman and offered her a ride home.

The students snapped their approval.

R.A. training also deals with the concept of healthy sex.

That's the focus of "Relationship Remix," a program devoted to discussing consent as the key to a positive sexual relationship. Since

2004, all incoming Michigan students have been required to attend the seminar.

When students returned to Ann Arbor earlier this month, Anna Forringer-Beal, 21, helped facilitate two Remix discussions for about 80 students. A major in anthropology and women's studies, Ms. Forringer-Beal is both a volunteer for Sapac, the organization that provides confidential help to victims of sexual assault and misconduct, and an R.A. for the second year in a row.

"We focused a lot on a scenario where someone you're interested in asks you to go back to their room," she said. "I tried to get at the idea that consenting to go back to the room is all you're consenting to. Some people see it as an innuendo. I tried to explain that direct communication is the best communication so there is no room for ambiguity."

No one in campus life underestimates how trying life as a resident adviser can be, even as the R.A.s acknowledge its satisfactions.

"Self-care is important," Ms. Hong said. "You can burn out. But we all try to take care of one another. Someone at Sapac might give me some chocolates with a note that says, 'Thank you for all you do,' or I'll get Facebook or text messages, 'I just want you to know you're a great person.' We all do that. We know how hard it can be, but we know how important these issues are."

Sex at Wesleyan: What's Changed, What Hasn't? An Alumna Asks

BY VANESSA GRIGORIADIS | AUG. 25, 2017

OVER 20 YEARS AGO, I drove to the small liberal arts college Wesleyan University in my parents' station wagon, a microwave-size computer and a dot-matrix printer in the trunk. Equally renowned for its academics and its social life, boasting alums like Santigold and Lin-Manuel Miranda, Wesleyan was and is a bastion of radical politics. In the 1990s, the school even inspired a Jeremy Piven comedy about trendy Gen X liberalism (Save the whales! Meat is murder! Gays in the military now!). That film has long since been forgotten, but the first two letters are on the lips of all Americans today: "PCU." Like many elite campuses, Wesleyan has more than doubled in price since then, with tuition and fees upward of $50,000 per year, and has been spit shined to brochure-worthy gloss. A sprawling $47 million student center has landed on the grounds, replacing a flying-saucer-shaped cafeteria with an affectionately remembered smoking area.

Yet courtesy of the 20-year nostalgia cycle, the students who will be dragging their luggage up dorm staircases next week will look almost the same. The quad will be awash in Dr. Martens boots, black chokers, Converse sneakers and shoulder-slung mini-backpacks. And not only do these kids look similar, they also talk, urgently, about many of the same issues. Like sex, consensual and not.

In the 1990s, my feminist friends and I had a fervent anti-sexual assault movement, including Take Back the Night marches down frat row and a list of guys to stay away from, furtively scribbled in a bathroom stall. We talked about sexual assault as an affront of the patriarchy, and universities did not like it. At Brown, originator of the bathroom list trend, an administrator smeared the authors as "Magic Marker terrorists" and threatened them with expulsion if caught.

As much as you may read about the angry cries of "social justice warriors" in current news, today's students discuss sexual assault in a completely new way. Their primary concern is sexual ethics. Debates about what is consensual and what is not, what type of sex is fair and what is immoral, are essential to life at Wesleyan, I learned during visits to the campus a few semesters ago. "There's a difference between illegal and unethical," Chloe, a neuroscience major, told me, firmly. "Life is not about doing whatever you can do. It's about not doing what is traumatic to another person."

What few older people see in today's "P.C." students is their overwhelming urge to be kind to each other. They may have spent their middle and high school years being bullied, or bullying others; for kids in their low-to-mid-teens, the internet is a bullying machine. But by college, their sense of morality has blossomed. And many adolescents want to sort the world categorically into good and bad, at once eager to draw boundaries and empathize with whatever others might possibly feel.

Adults may make fun of trigger warnings, but most kids support them because they're about extending a hand to others, undergirding an ethic of caring and decency. Calling out "micro-aggressions" among classmates and policing tone on social media appeal to them in much the same way. They don't understand why older people deride their generation as "crybullies," in the conservative publisher Roger Kimball's words, or as "fragile thugs," a phrase David Brooks, a New York Times columnist, has used.

It's like 1969 all over again, with smokeless vapes instead of gurgling bong hits; their stodgy, cynical, heartless parents won't give peace a chance. Sensitive kids of all stripes have joined this movement, including the type of student who would have gone on tour with Phish in the 1990s, or those who listened to moody emo bands like Taking Back Sunday in the 2000s.

Let's chalk up these kids' snarky, furiously penned essays for campus newspapers and meanspirited social media posts to the internet's mob mentality, a 20-year-old's clumsiness with rhetorical flourishes, and their deep need to be part of a clique. Political radicalism at college is now more vocation than avocation, and anyone who displays a trace of racism, misogyny or sexual predation is suspect.

In this climate, some people can become fiercely self-critical. One white male senior at Wesleyan, with luscious shoulder-length blond hair and wearing a prep's cable-knit sweater, described his discomfort to me. "I feel privileged, and I have a privilege," he said. "And I'm fine with girls on campus saying I have a privilege! I apologize that I was born into this form, but I am living the best I can." He chuckled, but then looked genuinely pained. "I'm not afraid to be me, but I don't want to come across as being insensitive."

This heightened ethical sensitivity is being applied to sexual intercourse, an activity whose standards have long been mutable and often lax. My mother's generation, coming of age in the 1970s, imagined that when a woman went to a man's apartment, she'd signaled her intent to have intercourse. Twenty years later, I thought I could walk out of that apartment without even an obligatory kiss, but I would never have lain down on a mattress with someone with whom I didn't plan to hook up. Today, inviting someone into your bed is "cuddling," usually but not always sexual, and certainly does not have to lead to intercourse.

These types of vague encounters most likely spurred the demand for some rules. Whereas my Gen X friends called weird, awkward and even predatory sexual experiences "bad nights," today's students use the label "sexual assault." If it feels violating, it is violating, and shouldn't be part of anyone's formative sexual experiences.

Notwithstanding the kind of talk that has come freely to the nation's current president, at today's Wesleyan a smack on the butt, a grab and kiss, and subjection to coercive speech like "I can't feel anything with a condom on" and "just a couple strokes" are considered potentially offensive and maybe actionable, often for the first time in history. Wesleyan's students were also not so impressed by my Take Back the Night stories, I was wounded to discover. "We don't want to change one night, we want to change every night," one of them told me, emphatically.

The much-mocked 1991 "Antioch Rules," meanwhile, now seem prescient. At Wesleyan, as at many American universities today — not only the Ivy League and some state universities, but other colleges in New York, California, Illinois and Connecticut — students are expected to abide by some form of an "affirmative consent" standard, colloquially called "yes means yes."

Silence can no longer be considered consent for sex. "No means no" misses the important question. Getting busy must include a verbal "yes" or some sort of totally-impossible-to-misinterpret moan or groan or high-pitched scream of pleasure. Also, this must be secured before every sexual act, from kissing to going all the way.

At some colleges, this way of having sex is considered ludicrous. At others, like Wesleyan, kids take it seriously. You can think of this the way they do — a high-toned, righteous issue about sexual autonomy — or as a novel courting ritual. It's not that different from sending an emoji to clarify one's meaning at the end of a text message.

Most students — and not only the type of aggressive liberal activist once called a "Magic Marker terrorist" — like these standards, perceiving them as a way of making sex more pleasurable instead of less. "It's attractive to me because he is showing me that he thinks I'm a person," said Karmenife, a talented writer from Harlem. "I'm not this receptacle. I'm not supposed to lie there and be his object. This is something that we're doing together."

Other students said the situation wasn't so simple. "Sometimes it's nice when guys ask more questions, sometimes it's weird," said a 21-year-old female student. "Some men in college are way too scared now of potentially assaulting people. I hooked up with a friend who was very drunk, and I was not very drunk. I liked him. Afterward he didn't like me. So I said, 'I'm upset, I liked you.' "

The young man reeled back, worrying that she was about to accuse him of assaulting her, not understanding that she was saying she was bummed he regarded the night as a drunken hookup and nothing more. "He was very upset about his level of drunkenness, and 'Did I take advantage of you?' I said, 'I'm not saying it was nonconsensual! I liked you.' " She added, in typical millennial patois, " 'You don't get to be the one, all worried Did I rape you? I'm upset about you passing the friendship line, and you're hyperventilating about your level of drunkenness!' "

As with all social etiquette, some people will take rules too far. These new sexual standards appeal to the ever-present undergraduate elimination of ambiguity. The need to communicate constantly — very millennial — may also be a naïve belief in explicitness. Nothing should be beyond words, no liminal realms of discomfort can be allowed to exist. But we can't lose sight of the fact that they're also about compassion. They're making sure that the desire of the other is present when gratifying oneself, an attunement to gratifying the other too.

One Saturday afternoon, I stopped by a narrow, chartreuse-painted condo on the outskirts of town. A handful of Wesleyan soccer players were in their driveway, basking in the sun and marking asphalt with chalk for the childhood game four square (they were using a hacky sack as a ball — hark, the 1990s!).

Between chatter about the mechanical failure of someone's Jeep, the relative merits of Wesleyan's lacrosse team and who was going to get the keg, I asked them about consent. Do their friends get it in sexual situations? "Um, that's weird," a student from Toms River, N.J., said, giving me side-eye and laughing. "I don't know what my friends ask or don't ask girls!"

But an economics major from Idaho cradling a Miller Light took a seat beside me. "On a personal level, I will always ask for consent — always! Regardless!" he said. "I say, 'Hey, is this O.K.? Are you O.K. with this?' It's awkward, yeah, but it's five seconds and it's over. And if the girl goes to Wesleyan, she recognizes what I'm doing: I'm asking for consent."

Soon one of his friends waved to him; it was his turn at four square. "I don't know what it will be like when I graduate from college, though," he said, tossing his beer into a garbage can like he was dunking a basketball.

"Am I still supposed to ask?" he said, walking away.

This article is adapted from **VANESSA GRIGORIADIS'S** book, "Blurred Lines: Rethinking Sex, Power & Consent on Campus."

45 Stories of Sex and Consent on Campus

BY THE NEW YORK TIMES | MAY 10, 2018

Editor's Note: The following accounts are selections from a collection of 45 testimonials published by The New York Times on May 10, 2018.

AS ANYONE WHO has fumbled through a sexual encounter knows, real-life sex can be far more complicated than a poster declaring, "Consent is Sexy." Many remain confused about what constitutes sexual consent, and talking about it in the moment can feel awkward. On college campuses, a combination of alcohol, inexperience and differing expectations about how one is "supposed" to perform only heightens the confusion.

In the time of #MeToo, the debate about how to handle sexual consent has become louder than ever. Many sexual encounters seem to take place in a so-called gray zone of miscommunication, denial, rationalization and, sometimes, regret.

We wanted to explore that complexity when we asked college students for their stories of navigating this gray zone: what they anticipated, how they negotiated consent and processed the aftermath, and what advice they would give their younger selves. These are their stories.

JESSICA BENNETT AND DANIEL JONES
A project of Modern Love and The New York Times Gender Initiative.

"You're laughing and flirting and you clearly want to hook up," he said. "You just don't want to admit it."

My curiosity and flirtation are not grounds to expect sex from me. I would love to be able to go out and enjoy myself without feeling self-conscious about whether or not I am "leading someone on."

FREYA, NEW ZEALAND

I remember being young, and overeager, and having no knowledge of sex but from porn. I never forced anyone to do anything, but I also know that I probably said things that could have made someone feel pressured. It was at an age where nothing ever went past making out and sending crude texts, but I still made mistakes.

Now, I've also been in a situation where I told someone I didn't want to have sex and then was heavily pressured to do so. I was far less sober than her, and said no.

"Whhhyyyyy," she said. "Please?"

That girl didn't force me to do anything, but I was still uncomfortable, and did things I didn't want to do.

I don't think it would be fair to call her a predator, because I know her well enough to know she would never want to hurt me. But at that point, does intent matter? She put me in a position I didn't want to be in, just as I am sure younger me put others in that position.

JACOB, CALIFORNIA

I had a hard time explaining what was wrong for a long time. I kissed her back when she kissed me. I never told her to stop. I couldn't find the words to tell my friends why I flinched when she touched me. She and I never talked while it was happening. Eventually I would stop moving, arms limp and eyes averted and focus on the crack in the ceiling of my room. She would continue, faster and harder, and sometimes when I would come back she would be done, and sometimes she wouldn't be. I don't think she ever noticed I was gone.

I wonder sometimes why I didn't say no, where all of my no's went every time I needed them.

JENNY, OHIO

Younger me was taught the mechanics of sex but nothing about what consent should look like. In other words, I knew how to give oral sex, but not how to refuse performing it. Entering the dating and hookup scene with low self-esteem and little knowledge led to many encounters of an "icky" nature: I didn't know how to stop them, once started, and often felt as if I was contractually obligated to take the guy to the end and expect nothing in return.

So I did, even as I wished I didn't have to.

LIVIA, NEW YORK

"I'm bad at saying no to people," a girl I hooked up with told me once. I don't remember exactly what began our conversation.

"In what situations?" I asked.

"Like … with men, when they want sex. I don't want to disappoint them, but I'm also not usually into it," she said.

"Do you remember a time that happened?"

"I mean … the last time I had sex with a guy, he was like, 'I don't have a condom, is that okay?' And I knew it wasn't, but I said yes anyway." She trailed off, looking unsure.

"Why did you say yes?"

"Because I didn't want him to be mad at me. Or yell at me. And I wasn't sure I didn't want it. I was already there, so I just let it happen." Her words hung in the air between us.

"You know that if you're ever not into something, I would rather have you tell me than have you be uncomfortable, right?" I said.

"Yeah. I know that with you," she said. "That's why I don't sleep with men anymore."

ELISE, CALIFORNIA

Early in our relationship when I brought up the subject of sex, she told me she had never done it before. I hadn't either, but I lied and said that I had had non-penetrative sex with a high school girlfriend. I lied so she would think I was more experienced. I lied to her so she would sleep with me. She did, and our sexual relationship was marked from then on as being between an experienced person and an inexperienced person.

SAM, IOWA

He was older. He had already graduated from university and had a job out of town, but was in town staying with a friend. I was excited; I'd never been on a date before. I picked the perfect outfit, shaved my legs and put on lipstick. He and his friend picked me up from my dorm and we drove to a gas station for alcohol. He bought a large bottle of gin.

As the afternoon went on, we drank, smoked, drank, talked and drank. By the end of the night, I just wanted to be in a bed — either mine or his. He asked if I would go home with him. I said yes. I stumbled to the guest bedroom. I took my clothes off. He turned the lights off and got on top of me.

"What do you want me to do to you?"

I shrugged.

At first it was enjoyable, fun even. But then the alcohol kicked in more, and all I could do was lie there, trying not to puke. He didn't seem to notice.

In the weeks after, he sent me several text messages asking to meet up. I deleted them without responding. I still couldn't process what had happened. I never said no, but I never really said yes, either.

A.A., MISSOURI

"Niñas bien," meaning "good girls," do not have casual sex unless you have a serious boyfriend or a husband. "Niñas bien" do have sex, but it is not something you tell people, nor do you brag about it much. It's more like a dirty little secret.

I was going on dates with an older "niño bien" ("good boy") from my university. He invited me over to his cousin's house for a party. In advance, this boy told me that perhaps it was better if I slept over because we were going to drink, and it wasn't safe to venture home in the middle of the night. I trusted him.

The party was not a party, more like a gathering of five strangers. We drank, we smoked, we kissed, then suddenly everybody left. "Good boy" took me to the bedroom. We kissed first, then he started pulling off my clothes — quickly, as if he had eight hands. He said how much and for how long he had wanted me like this, how much he fancied me. I liked him too. Part of me was happy to hear that, to see I could turn a boy into pieces of desire.

The moment turned bittersweet because I started to fear that if we went all the way, everything would turn just sexual. I didn't feel ready to have sex with him yet. It was 3 a.m. I felt guilty for being so naïve and I feared his reaction if I said no. To this day I look back with regret and shame for being so naïve.

ANA, MEXICO

Alcohol was my unlimited get-out-of-jail-free card. With the newness of intoxication as an excuse, I could flirt without repercussion, embrace my nascent sexuality without consequence. So when the boy answered the door and invited me in to watch a movie, I agreed, thinking, "What's the harm in that? Nothing serious will happen with his roommate there."

We were several minutes into the film when he started rubbing my shoulders and muttered, "Is this okay?" in my ear.

A strange concoction of guilt and arousal descended over me and I tensed. I knew I shouldn't be doing this. I knew under different circumstances I wouldn't be doing this. But at the same time, my mind foggy and clouded, I didn't know if I wanted him to stop. "Um … yes?" I whispered back.

The boy's hands trailed from my back, circling forward to a place my mother referred to as the "husband-only zone." And suddenly, I started to feel queasy.

"And this?" he asked.

I was silent for longer this time, before the word "yeah" emerged in a nervous high-pitched squeak.

He started to fumble with my buttons, hands grazing over my racing heart.

You've let it go too far now, I thought. It would be rude to stop him. Besides, you felt good before. Maybe it will get better?

MEAGHAN, NEW YORK

10:04 p.m.: We're walking, hand-in-hand, back to my dorm room. We're joking around with each other and laughing.

10:10 p.m.: I wrestle with my key to open the door to my room. I turn the lights on and draw the blinds. You wrap your arms around me and kiss my cheek. I'm incredibly happy ... but also very drunk.

10:13 p.m.: I turn around and kiss you. I take my socks off and ask you to turn the lights off.

10:15 p.m.: You run your hands down my sides, a sign that you want to have sex. I tell you I'm way too drunk and I'll probably throw up. I try to hug you instead so we can go to sleep.

10:17 p.m.: You're still running your hands all over me and trying to take my clothes off. I push your hand away and tell you again that I'm drunk. You laugh and kiss my forehead. You kiss my neck — you know it's my weakness. I let you take my shirt off but tell you I still don't want to have sex.

10:20 p.m.: I say no but my will is crumbling ... I'm too drunk to say anything. You say you love me and I should do this for you. You beg. I say "fine," on the verge of falling asleep.

10:20 a.m.: "Get out," I whisper, trembling. You think I'm being dramatic. You don't think you did anything wrong.

N.M., OHIO

Whenever I start a new relationship, I always ask what specific things they're comfortable with and when they're comfortable with them.

The tough part for me isn't having conversations and being clear about understanding boundaries.

The tough part is realizing that no matter how careful you are to ensure that there's consent there's always the thought in the back of your mind that you're letting someone into a space where they could very easily make your life a living hell if they felt the inclination. My friends and I often joke that we need to make a sex tape every time to prove that everything was consensual, because it's scary when you think about the consequences that could ride on your word versus someone else's.

CLARK, MICHIGAN

On a September night, I woke up naked on a couch in a room I did not know. I was confused and throwing up into a wine glass. He walked in wearing a robe and sat down. I had to ask if we had sex, and he said yes. I had to ask if we used a condom, and he promised yes. All the stories I had heard of sexual assault were flooding my mind, and out of panic, I acted. I told myself: "This could not happen to me." So we had sex again. This time I was conscious.

That next day I was googling "blackout sex" and "was I sexually assaulted" with shaking fingers. That same night he texted, "Also dinner this week," asking to get together.

I asked to meet so I could fill the holes in my memory. He looked as if he were about to cry, or vomit, when I explained how little I remembered. We left it at that.

Within weeks, we ran into each other, and he drunkenly told me how he liked me. He asked to go on a real date.

We went on that date, did homework together each week, made plans, ate dinner in the dining hall, and looked at memes on that same couch I had woken up on several weeks earlier. One night he asked me to be his girlfriend; another night he told me he loved me. He even suggested meeting my parents.

If he liked me, it wasn't sexual assault, right?

But suddenly he stopped answering and we never spoke again — as if nothing had happened.

SYDNEY, VIRGINIA

I was so embarrassed. There I was: a little freshman, naked in a senior's bed. Obviously I had to have led him on if he just assumed we were going to have sex! I could have gotten dressed and left — he wasn't asking for an explanation, and frankly he wouldn't have cared. He also would not have stopped me. But I was so ashamed to have put myself in that situation that I felt as if I had to go through with it. So I did.

It was physically painful in the moment and emotionally painful the following days and weeks. When it was over, I tried to pick up some of the pieces of my shattered pride and insisted that I spend the night (at least maybe he would want to cuddle, right?). I ended up sneaking out an hour after he fell asleep and never spoke to him again.

YAEL, CALIFORNIA

I weighed my options at the moment. It'll be over in two minutes. That's not that bad, I thought. So I just zoned out. I just stared at the ticking clock in my room. 103 seconds. 1.71 minutes.

262,800 minutes later, and I still find myself questioning the consensuality of the interaction. Should I have spoken up more? Should he have listened to my original cue telling him I didn't like that? How do men know the difference between a girl who is teasing them and one who is trying to avert behavior?

TINA, CANADA

I was in the dorm room of a man I considered a close friend when he asked me, "Why can you hook up with other people, but you won't with me?"

I wanted to say, "Because it's my body," but I didn't. I should have said, "Because I don't feel that way about you." He was my friend. I

I thought he would pass out immediately, and we would laugh about it in the morning. Then he unzipped his pants and placed my hand inside.

"What's wrong?" he asked as I tried to move my hand away.

"You're drunk, and I don't want to do this. You'll regret this in the morning."

"I won't regret it," he said. "C'mon."

"No."

When I woke up in the morning, he was gone. We set up a time to talk later that day, and I told him how he took advantage of me. Tears streamed down his face as he asked me if he was a rapist now. "I'm sorry," he said. "I'm sorry."

I rubbed his back for the last time. He lifted one of his hands and waved me off, a don't-forgive-me gesture for all the things he could control but hadn't. We never spoke again. I don't know if we ever will.

MARIA, ILLINOIS

The Weinstein Effect and the #MeToo movement have forced a whole generation of university men to look inward and ask themselves: Am I hardwired to only want sex? I wracked my brain for instances where I might have crossed a line. I considered my sexual history to be relatively respectful and vanilla, always asking before moving forward. But there was one time I couldn't shake.

I was on the way back from a party with a friend when we stopped at my room, kissed and she followed me in. We woke up the next day on my single bed in a naked embrace. We'd had sex, but I didn't remember all of it, most importantly, asking for her consent.

We exchanged texts after, saying we were both drunk and it was kind of O.K. But two years later, in the midst of MeToo, her messages took on a new meaning, and I was filled with dread. Rather than let these feelings fester, I needed to speak to her about it in person. We had been on friendly terms ever since, but we never brought up what happened that night.

So I asked her to meet for lunch, and as we were wrapping up, I blurted out the question whose answer I dreaded the most: "Did I cross a line?"

She was surprised. "No, you didn't do anything wrong," she said with a smile. "But thanks for asking."

JAMES, PENNSYLVANIA

I always thought I wouldn't hesitate to speak up if I felt uncomfortable in an intimate situation. But at 1 a.m on a Saturday with a shirtless sophomore, I cared more about how to politely make him leave than standing up for myself. A week prior, we'd matched on Tinder, sporadically texting, half-heartedly trying to make plans. When we finally did, after a campus party, I found myself trying to think of ways to end the night while protecting his dignity, immediately regretting my decision to meet up.

Within thirty seconds of entering my room, he started kissing me aggressively. I kissed back for a minute, then recoiled. He leaned in. I let him. He started unbuttoning my shirt. Alarm bells rang in my brain. I shifted my position and his hand fell away. "Sorry, I'm not really a hookup kind of person," I said, despite all evidence to the contrary. I'd found previous hookups empowering in the moment but ultimately unsatisfying. I didn't know why I'd gone down that road again when it wasn't what I wanted.

"Okay," he said. "Just talking is fun too."

I doubted that was what he really thought. Our talk was interjected with kissing. He made me uncomfortable with his forcefulness, yet he hadn't done anything that would constitute sexual assault. I had invited him over and kissed him back. But if he hadn't technically done anything wrong, why did I feel so terrible?

CAITLIN, CALIFORNIA

I don't remember taking our clothes off, making out or sensually touching. I just came to and we were having sex. It was jarring.

We had been flirting all semester and there was almost an expectation for us to hook up. However, she knew that I was too intoxicated that night to give consent. She had seen me throwing up in my bathroom and even had a conversation with my best friend where he told her that we shouldn't hook up tonight. She agreed.

Yet later we did. I don't feel traumatized, invaded or used. More than anything, I just feel uncomfortable about it all. Once I came to, I tried to roll with it, but I wasn't feeling hot. I just wanted to take a shower really.

I know she didn't have bad intentions, yet she did take advantage of the state I was in. So should I tell her that? I don't want to. I just know there would be so much unwanted fallout, prolonging a situation that I want to get behind me. No harm, no foul, right?

JAMES, LOUISIANA

My sexual assailant and I have identical breakfast routines. He's like a ghost, my personal haunting — appropriate, since ghosts linger in places where they shouldn't.

What did I do to deserve this? I always thought that my sin was my silence; he lingers on campus because I am keeping him here by failing to speak up.

Years ago, on Halloween, my sexual assailant grabbed my butt, stuck his hands up my shirt and put his arm around my throat. I was wearing a "Risky Business" costume, boxer shorts and a white Oxford, and the ghost reached in, up, and around while I realized that my workout routine had not made me strong.

"Do not kiss me again — you're bad at it," I said.

"Then I have to practice."

Tongue down throat.

Two years later, a different boy asked me permission before every move. "Can I touch you here?" "Yes." "Can I kiss you?" "Yes." "Can I take off your shirt?" "No."

Pointed look, eye roll, come on. Yes? I said yes until I was naked, save socks, and I never wanted to be and wasn't sure how it happened. I exploded into tears — a tried-and-true method for getting a boy to stop trying to have sex with me. I biked away from his fraternity at 2 a.m.

Because he was still my friend, I told him a few days later about yet another boy I was fascinated by because, "He stopped me from going down on him because he said I was too drunk to consent."

"So you like him ... because he didn't rape you? That's the standard?"

I don't know what I said, but I know what I didn't say: "Better than what I got from you."

Like I never told on my ghost, I never told my friend who he really was. I never told him that he, question-asker and yes-receiver, does not understand consent at all. And I don't know who I think I'm sparing with my silence. I'm certainly not sparing me.

MADELINE, NEW HAMPSHIRE

It's hard for me to put a label on what happened. Sexual assault (too harsh?), rape (way too harsh?), a nonconsensual first time (too kind?), a misunderstanding (way too kind?). He stopped when I asked him to. But he started in the first place.

I know that what happened with us would have seemed normal and consensual in many relationships. I know it would have seemed like I wanted it from the way I was acting. But I had never had sex before and didn't understand.

I was naïve, a prude, a tease by most people's definition, still holding onto the possibility that I would wait until marriage, even though we often found ourselves in bed with barely any clothes on. Before, we had always stopped short of sex. I trusted him to not go further. That night, he was on top of me and I enjoyed him there until I felt something I hadn't before.

Was this sex? Of course not, I told myself. Sex is supposed to hurt the first time. But maybe I was more drunk than I realized. It began to dawn on me what was happening. I said no, pushed him off. At first, my body screamed that what happened was not okay. But over time I normalized it and buried it. It was years before I began to unpack what happened.

That night, as I lay there crying, he told me that it wasn't sex, that he was barely inside me. But it was sex. And I didn't want it. I wasn't asked. I hadn't said yes.

GABRIELA, INDIANA

One night she came over to my dorm room and we started to make out. Shortly after we started, she made it clear she only wanted to watch a show on Netflix and sleep. Wanting more, I kept kissing her and touching her, but when she reiterated that she wasn't into it, I stopped. When I thought she was asleep, I masturbated next to her, grabbing at her body while I did. Shortly after, she got up and said she wanted to go back to her dorm. I said good night and thought little of it.

A year later, as the #MeToo movement began to take form and especially after Aziz Ansari's story broke, I started to question my actions in that moment and in others. I started to see that while I believed I had always been respectful and obtained consent, my sex life involved many incidences of pressuring women into sexual acts until they relented. I haven't talked to the girl I knew a year ago since that night, although I occasionally see her around campus. Sometimes I want to go to her and apologize, but really I have no idea how she feels about the situation or if she even remembers me at all.

C.P., CONNECTICUT

The night we had sex, his kisses left my chin slick with saliva, an oral technique best described as "slurping." A few days later, he asked to see me again, so I texted: "this isn't what I'm looking for at the moment." The truth was, he wasn't what I was looking for at any moment.

In the weeks after, I wondered why I hadn't spoken up. If I wasn't enjoying myself, why hadn't I told him to stop? Why hadn't I just said no?

He was a grad student and I was an undergraduate. We were both Asian American. Our dynamic was fraught with factors that left me inclined to stay quiet. I told myself these things like I was delivering an inspirational TED talk: It isn't your fault! Blame social constructs! You are valid! But I can't help but feel that it was my fault. I was sober, informed, capable of leaving. Yes, there were reasons I didn't say no, but I could have. I should have.

I think I wanted to maintain the persona I had created. I had chosen the role of a confident, sex-positive feminist. I paid for my dinner. I kissed him first. By the time clothes were shed, it would've been awkward to stop. I didn't want to be labeled a prude, a tease.

More than anything, I was scared. Scared that I would say stop and he wouldn't, and then I would know for sure it was rape. In my fear, I convinced myself that bad sex was an inevitability that wasn't worth making a fuss about. As long as I didn't say anything, I could rationalize and minimize my discomfort.

LEANNE, OKLAHOMA

My significant other recently asked me how many sexual partners I've had, or what my "number" was. I didn't tell him. Not because I am ashamed — I know my worth is not dependent on how much or how little sex I have had — but because I'm unsure how to count them.

Like many young adults, I keep a list; names, descriptions and, for mine, a 5-star rating system. So I had a solid numerical answer prepared for his question. But I didn't respond because I don't know how to answer that anymore. The older I become, the more I have come to realize that most, if not all, of my sexual encounters have been in a murky "gray zone" of consent.

Do I include non-consensual partners in my total? What about ones where I initiated it and then just lay there until it ended because I realized I didn't actually want it, but, oops, too late to back out now? Does including nights where I drunkenly woke up to someone on top of me add to my total?

I didn't know what affirmative consent was. I didn't know I had the option to say no. I thought unenjoyable sex was the norm. It's just kissing and fumbling and next thing you know, you're having sex, and you're thinking "ohmygod this guy is so bad, this doesn't really feel all that amazing like but it looks like he's enjoying himself; I just hope we can get this over with fast because I have a test to study for."

The absence of 'no' does not equal 'yes.' I wish I had known that when I was first discovering my sexuality.

NIKKI, MINNESOTA

I hate admitting how much sex I've had because it was "polite" to just let him finish. You read stories of rape and sexual assault but never about your own manners pressuring you into having sex. Sometimes you just don't want to have sex after all the buildup but there is no way to get out of it without coming off as rude or disappointing your partner, who is probably a good person, not some creepy dude in a club.

When I was 18 I actually did say no to a guy mid-hookup. My friend, her boyfriend, and I went to the house of one of his friends. After much alcohol consumption, my friend and her boyfriend left to have sex. I wasn't uncomfortable. The other guy was good looking, and fun to talk to. When he pulled me onto his lap and kissed me, it felt nice. When he suggested we move to his bedroom, I thought, "Why not? There's nothing else to do." What was I supposed to do, say no and awkwardly sit there with him while I waited for my friend to emerge?

Soon we were naked and he was searching for a condom, until finally I said, "No, not tonight." He looked surprised, then laughed and said, "Let me change your mind," and kissed me. I kissed him back. I'd already been doing that, so how could I refuse? But finally I pushed him away and said "If you have to convince someone to have sex, something's wrong."

RACHEL, NEW YORK

CHAPTER 3

Looking for Solutions

In response to the wave of sexual assaults, there has been a nationwide search for solutions. Universities, state governments and individuals have been brainstorming how to create a system of consent that delineates between consensual and nonconsensual encounters, turning something that is often gray into black and white. The articles in this chapter show the steps that have been taken to improve sexual consent policies and the obstacles these practices face.

Consent in the Digital Age: Can Apps Solve a Very Human Problem?

BY MAYA SALAM | MARCH 2, 2018

"NO MEANS NO" began to give way to "yes means yes" as the credo of sexual consent decades ago, but the shift has been swiftly propelled in recent years by legislation and, most recently, by the #MeToo and #TimesUp movements.

The concept of affirmative consent — the act of giving verbal permission clearly and often during intimate encounters — was pioneered at Antioch College, where an affirmative sexual consent policy was instituted in 1990. It was widely mocked then, but similar policies have since spread to campuses nationwide, and today, the concept is acknowledged well beyond university grounds.

Now, apps aiming to help partners mitigate confusion in the bedroom have emerged, the newest of which approaches consent like a legal contract. LegalFling, which was introduced to users in beta on Monday, lets users give explicit sexual consent via an agreement, or a "live contract," a dynamic document that users can continuously interact with and update.

And yes, these agreements could hold up in court, said Andrew D. Cherkasky, a former special victims prosecutor who now handles dozens of felony-level sexual assault cases each year as a criminal defense attorney. He emphasized, however, that what LegalFling offers are not technically contracts, but documentations of intent, which are legally viable.

LegalFling aims to make the sexual dos and don'ts explicit in a "fun and clear way," according to its website.

Condom use, bondage, dirty talk, sexting: the app lets users set their boundaries before an encounter — boundaries that can be adjusted at any time with a tap and shared with a potential partner. (Sound familiar? Netflix's twisted-tech series "Black Mirror" incorporated a similar transaction in its episode "Hang the DJ.")

"A profile update is an event we store on the blockchain and will subsequently update the live contract," Rick Schmitz, a co-creator of LegalFling, recently said. The transaction is encrypted, timestamped and stored. (A blockchain is a collection of digital transactions that are registered in a sequence of "blocks" of data.)

Will these apps revolutionize sex? Not likely. As complex human beings with ever-changing desires, we may not fit so neatly into click-and-consent existence portrayed in that "Black Mirror" episode, or envisioned by the app developers. But they are making steps toward addressing a problem that needs solving.

WHEN YES BECOMES NO.

Dr. Michelle Drouin, a leading expert on technology and relationships, said the apps are good at documenting consent, but don't account much for fluctuating human emotions. They don't necessarily allow for any immediacy of one's feelings, she said.

Use of the app "has to be planned," she said, "and it's really difficult for us to even know how we feel in the present moment, much less trying to anticipate how we might feel an hour from now."

Mr. Schmitz said that a LegalFling agreement does not override someone changing his or her mind in the moment or being too intoxicated, for example, to consent. The company suggests you withdraw consent via the app at that moment, but, of course, that's not always possible.

If encounters leave users feeling violated, Mr. Schmitz said, they should notify the aggressor afterward in a message, and it will be added to the record.

Also possible with a tap: triggering cease-and-desist letters, according to the website.

The creators of LegalFling, part of the blockchain company LegalThings, which digitized regulation for the Dutch government, said they decided to apply their technology to sexual consent when, in December, Sweden proposed a law that would require people to get explicit verbal consent before sexual contact.

But Dr. Drouin is not sold on apps as a solution to a very human problem. The requirement to interact with an app during a sexual encounter is "completely unrealistic," she said.

"It would be very awkward within the context of an intimate encounter to be like, 'Wait a second, I'm changing my mind on the app and also with you,' " she said.

More important, she said, the app could persuade someone to fulfill acts simply because they agreed to them in advance, or to overcommit in an effort to appear more sexually adventurous.

LEGITIMATE, BUT THERE ARE CAVEATS.

These digital agreements could certainly be used as evidence of, at the time the button was pushed, what an individual's intent or desires were, according to Mr. Cherkasky. "We already see it all the time in social media or text messages," he said, adding that they would most likely be legally viable in cases globally, as well.

But these agreements do have the potential to be used as a means of protection to an aggressor, he said, especially by a violent and pre-meditating criminal. It's very common in domestic violence cases for an attacker to have a "great deal of power over the person and force them to do a number of things," he said.

Even implying that someone doesn't have the right to change their mind is a real risk, he said. Though the risk also exists for an accused person, who may have fully gotten consent in the moment even if "the box wasn't checked."

"It turns consent into a joke, a technicality that people think is black and white or can be recorded in a moment of time," he said.

But technology is reflecting a cultural shift in respecting and understanding the idea of consent, he said.

Dr. Drouin agreed: People are now communicating about these incidents in ways that are recordable and admissible in court, she said. "It's no longer 'he said, she said.' "

AN APP WITH A DIFFERENT LENS.

While LegalFling is the newest app hoping to address the rising tide of consent awareness, it's not the first. We-Consent, introduced in 2015 by the nonprofit Institute for the Study of Coherence and Emergence, was created for students on college campuses to help them adhere to the implementation of affirmative consent rules.

In 2014, California became the first state to require colleges to use affirmative consent as the standard in disciplinary decisions, which inspired the creation of We-Consent, said Michael Lissack, director of the institute.

We-Consent records a short video of two people stating their affir-mative consent, according to the company, and uses facial recognition technology. That recording is encrypted and inaccessible without a legal petition.

There are over 100,000 encrypted files, Mr. Lissack said, but the institute has had only two requests ever to retrieve the videos. In both instances — before We-Consent turned in the videos — the fact that they were available spurred the cases to settle, Mr. Lissack said.

"From Day 1, the purpose of the app was to get people who are about do something to discuss what they're going to do with one another," he said.

Consent can happen only from discussion, he said, "not from sending emoji back and forth, nodding your head or signing some weird legal agreement."

The Trouble With Sex Robots

OPINION | BY LAURA BATES | JULY 17, 2017

LONDON — Frigid Farrah. That's the imaginatively alliterative name of the sex robot that's yours to rape for just $9,995. Or rather, that's the name of the "personality" you would set your Roxxxy TrueCompanion robot to if you wanted to find her not too "appreciative" when you "touched her in a private area," according to the company's website.

Sex robots are coming, warns a new report from the Foundation for Responsible Robotics. Indeed, many are already available and shipping worldwide.

This is not a niche issue. A 2016 study by the University of Duisburg-Essen in Germany found that more than 40 percent of the 263 heterosexual men surveyed said they could imagine using a sex robot. One company, the California-based Abyss Creations, already ships up to 600 hyper-realistic sex dolls per year to customers worldwide.

Frigid Farrah is not alone in providing her user with a replica of a human partner without the nagging complication of consent. According to the website of Lumi Dolls, the company that operated a short-lived sex doll brothel in Barcelona earlier this year, the dolls allow the user to "set the limits and she will let herself be taken along for the ride — she's the perfect submissive partner."

One of the authors of the Foundation for Responsible Robotics report, Noel Sharkey, a professor of artificial intelligence and robotics at the University of Sheffield, England, said there are ethical arguments within the field about sex robots with "frigid" settings.

"The idea is robots would resist your sexual advances so that you could rape them," Professor Sharkey said. "Some people say it's better they rape robots than rape real people. There are other people saying this would just encourage rapists more."

Like the argument that women-only train compartments are an answer to sexual harassment and assault, the notion that sex robots could reduce rape is deeply flawed. It suggests that male violence against women is innate and inevitable, and can be only mitigated, not prevented. This is not only insulting to a vast majority of men, but it also entirely shifts responsibility for dealing with these crimes onto their victims — women, and society at large — while creating impunity for perpetrators.

Rape is not an act of sexual passion. It is a violent crime. We should no more be encouraging rapists to find a supposedly safe outlet for it than we should facilitate murderers by giving them realistic, blood-spurting dummies to stab. Since that suggestion sounds ridiculous, why does the idea of providing sexual abusers with lifelike robotic victims sound feasible to some?

Because we live in a society that still fails to see sexual violence for the crime it is.

To make such a solution available is to risk normalizing rape by giving it a publicly acceptable face. Research has shown that heterosexual men who are exposed to pornography and men's lifestyle magazines and reality TV programs that objectify women are more likely to be accepting of violence against women. In a world in which you can sleep with a prostitute and then murder her in the video game Grand Theft Auto, sex robots are misogynistic wish fulfillments.

While there have been calls for child sex robots to be banned from Britain, no one seems to be advocating a similar policy for their adult female counterparts. This seems simple enough: It is illegal to have sex with a child, but not with an adult woman, after all. But it is also illegal to have sex with an adult woman who does not consent, and consenting is not something these robots are capable of.

That doesn't matter, the argument goes, because these are not women, but animatronic objects, so consent is not necessary. The same reasoning is used to deflect fears that such robots could influence societal attitudes toward women. "She's not a someone. She is a machine," their creators are quick to respond when questions of moral ambiguity are raised. "Is it ethically dubious to force my toaster to make my toast?"

"If women can have a vibrator," the TrueCompanion website asks smoothly, "why can't men have a Roxxxy? Having a sex robot is just another 'aid' that allows both women and men to make their dreams become reality."

This is disingenuous when the robots' makers' deliberate aim is to replicate real women as closely as possible. These are no toasters. "She has touches so realistic," Lumi Dolls enthuses about its Lily model, "that at times you can hardly distinguish her from a real woman."

Yes, sex aids have long existed, but sex robots position women as toys, women as objects for men to play with. By making these robots as realistic as possible — from self-warming models to those that speak and suck, from some with a pulse to others that flirt with their owners — their creators are selling far more than an inanimate sex aid. They are effectively reproducing real women, complete with everything, except autonomy.

Some examples seem explicitly designed to mimic scenarios in which real-life women might be less likely to give consent. Want to have sex with a schoolgirl, or a woman dressed for the workplace or the gym? There's a lifelike doll for all of that.

Ambiguous descriptors like "African" and "small Asian figure" sit alongside "submissive" and "party girl" personalities, playing into sexualized racist stereotypes. A doll dressed as a geisha dispenses drinks when you squeeze its right breast.

The production of these dolls and robots, a great majority of which are female, cannot be disentangled from the stark gender inequality of the world in which they are produced. It is no coincidence that Real-Doll estimates that fewer than 5 percent of its customers are women. The issue is not whether a sex robot, as an abstract concept, could be useful or harmful, but the impact of making such robots available in a society that already subjugates, discriminates against, and physically and sexually abuses women.

Already there are hints of how such products could play into the wider backdrop of violation and harassment of women. Last year, a

Hong Kong designer made headlines for creating a robotic version of the actor Scarlett Johansson without her permission. RealDoll explains on its website that it is illegal to create exact replicas of women without their consent but adds, "We can, however, use photographs of a person of your choice to select a face structure as similar as possible from our line of 16 standard female faces." The site boasts, "We have done this with good success in the past." This is significant, considering that an estimated 15 percent of American women have been victims of stalking.

"There's a basic human right that everybody's entitled to a sexual life," Professor Sharkey said. But is the basic human right to a sexual life the same as a universal entitlement to a young, attractive woman? Because that is what it is being subverted into here.

There is a big difference between the right to dignity and privacy, the right to consensual sexual activity, and the idea that every man has some fundamental right to a woman's body. By replicating women as realistically as possible, this is what such robots attempt to provide — down to every detail except the pesky necessity for an actual woman's consent.

LAURA BATES, the founder of the Everyday Sexism Project, is the author, most recently, of "Girl Up."

Equipping Women to Stop Campus Rape

OPINION | BY TINA ROSENBERG | MAY 30, 2018

BERTA FELIX was a junior at Florida Atlantic University in Boca Raton in the fall of 2016. Around Christmas, she went out for drinks with a male friend. Ms. Felix did not consider it a date. Her friend did, apparently. He insisted on paying for the drinks. He drove her home, and in her front yard, he started kissing her.

"I don't want this," she recalled telling him.

"I paid for the drinks," he said. "I thought you wanted to go out and have fun." He continued to kiss her.

Ms. Felix slapped him, jabbed her elbow in his stomach, and marched into her house.

She reacted the way she did because she had just completed a new 12-hour sexual assault-reduction course at Florida Atlantic, called Flip the Script. Among other lessons, Flip the Script teaches that acquaintances, not strangers, pose the greatest risk; how to recognize the warning signs of coercion that often precede assault; and how to respond effectively.

Ms. Felix didn't miss the warning. "If I hadn't taken the course, I would not have caught the signs," she said. "We were in the driveway of my house and I had my keys in hand. He could have persisted, come in and carried on."

Ms. Felix has not had to employ her Flip the Script lessons again, but she remains an enthusiast. She originally took the course just to get involved in something. But she liked it so much she took it again — and again. "It was an eye-opener, and every time I learn something new," she said. Now that she's going back for graduate school, she wants to take Flip the Script a fourth time.

An undergraduate woman has a greater than one-in-10 chance of experiencing rape or attempted rape — it's a huge issue on every

Graduating students from Stanford University protested campus rape in 2016.

campus — and nothing tried so far has worked very well to reduce sexual assault overall.

That makes the extraordinary results of Flip the Script particularly welcome. In one study, participants in the program were victims of 46 percent fewer rapes than a control group, and two-thirds fewer attempted rapes — which means that women were able to head off trouble at a very early stage.

Two years after the course ended, the results still held for attempted rape, while rapes were 31 percent lower than in the control group.

Those results are especially impressive because the study was very strong — a randomized control trial carried out with 893 female students at three Canadian universities. Evidence-Based Programs, a website that evaluates research, cites Flip the Script as one of only 10 programs in any field that it has placed in its Top Tier — the only one in violence prevention that made the grade.

One school that tested it is the University of Windsor in Ontario, where the program's author, Charlene Senn, is a professor of psychology and of women's and gender studies. Dr. Senn built the program on top of an older and shorter course named Assess, Acknowledge and Act. Later, Sarah Deatherage-Rauzin, the health promotion coordinator at Florida Atlantic, called its successor Flip the Script, and that's what a lot of universities call it now.

Flip the Script trains only women (including all people who identify as women). Here's what it teaches them:

The perpetrator of a sexual assault — and only the perpetrator — is at fault.

"People think, 'Oh, she's dressing that kind of way,' " Ms. Felix said. "We learned it is never a woman's fault if she is raped."

Most sexual assaults are committed by someone the victim knows.

"The creep in the bushes is not reality," said Abigail Brickley, a student at the University of Iowa who said that participants found this one of the most surprising revelations of the class. "You are most likely to be attacked by someone you already have some sort of relationship with — an acquaintance or friend."

That makes it harder to respond. "Shock, disbelief and questioning of our own perceptions are normal reactions, but they delay our acknowledgment of the danger and our action," said Dr. Senn.

Most sexual assaults take place in private.

Only 17 percent occur with a third person present. So training bystanders to intervene, although useful, has limited value.

Sexual assault often presents early warning signs.

"Like somebody who tries to separate you from the group, who's very persistent in insisting you get another drink or he drive you somewhere," said Ms. Brickley. "Like not taking no for an answer."

Women are socialized to not resist sexual assault.

"It's the feeling, 'I have to be nice. I don't want to offend this person,' " said Dusty Johnstone, the sexual misconduct and prevention officer at the University of Windsor; she runs the program there. "All the ways women are socialized dampen their ability to resist."

Crying and pleading do not work very well.

"The most effective responses are loud and obnoxious," said Dr. Johnstone. "We teach women to breathe and to yell. Yelling gives you energy. Use that verbal forcefulness, and if that doesn't work, physical force." The program spends an hour on verbal response and two hours on physical self-defense.

Dr. Senn had concluded that there was something missing in the original Assess, Acknowledge and Act program: Women need to be clear about their own desires and boundaries. What do I like? What do I want to do with this person? What would I never consider doing?

"Sexual assault often starts with verbal coercive pressure," she said, with assailants telling their victims, "Other women would do this," "What kind of a prude are you if you won't do this?"

"When you know your own desires, the pressure being applied is much more visible to you much more quickly," she said. "You don't spend time thinking: 'Maybe I am just inexperienced. Maybe that wouldn't be so bad.' You can say, 'I don't want that,' and it becomes really obvious faster that it's a danger."

So she added a unit on sexuality and relationships, using a curriculum called Our Whole Lives.

She tested the course with the sexuality unit, and without it. It worked better with.

If something cuts the risk of rape by nearly half, you'd think universities would be eager to put it to use. But Dr. Senn said that only 10 schools are using it — seven in Canada, one in New Zealand and two in the United States, (Florida Atlantic was the first in the United States, followed by the University of Iowa). Ten more schools — in Canada, Australia and the United States — are in the process of starting.

Ms. Deatherage-Rauzin said that a year after their training, only one woman among Florida Atlantic's nearly 100 participants said she had needed to use the physical defense strategies. Several women reported using the techniques short of physical self-defense. None had been raped.

One challenge is enrollment; 100 students isn't many, out of Florida Atlantic's 30,000. "Most students are commuters here," said Ms. Deatherage-Rauzin. "It's a 12-hour program. Getting them to commit to come to campus for after-hours events is a little difficult."

When the study of the program was being conducted at Windsor, it came with funds to help the school recruit participants. Now the school tries to find other ways. "We've even given away French fries," said Dr. Johnstone, to encourage women to spend a few minutes listening to the recruiting pitch.

The small enrollment level has made Flip the Script relatively expensive — $250 per participant, according to Evidence-Based Programs. But that is expected to drop, because it includes giving facilitators training — a one-time expense — and word-of-mouth might increase participation.

Flip the Script and other programs that work exclusively with women differ with the approach most universities are now adopting, which is working with bystanders — essentially, treating everyone as a potential ally in stopping sexual violence. Many bystander programs (such as Green Dot and Bringing In the Bystander) do work to shift attitudes and increase bystander intervention. Over the long term, they can change social norms, which is crucial. But they're not enough in the short term, given that so few sexual assaults are committed in the presence of third parties.

Many colleges also require entering students to do short online or in-person trainings on sexual consent and on alcohol — by far the most prevalent date-rape drug, involved in 96 percent of college sexual assaults. (Here's one novel program that reduces heavy drinking on campus by telling students how much their peers really drink.)

What about teaching men not to rape? Great idea! But we don't know how. "By the time they're in mid- to late adolescence, their sexual scripts and view of masculinity are pretty fixed," said Rory Newlands, a researcher on sexual violence at the University of Nevada, Reno. The only programs for males that show effects so far, for example Safe Dates, work with middle-school boys.

Ms. Deatherage-Rauzin said that when she first read the research on Dr. Senn's program she was impressed, but hesitated to try it. Training women to reduce their risk has been seen as telling women: "Rape is your fault for not acting like a 'good girl.' "

"At the time, the Centers for Disease Control and the American College Health Association were not recommending risk reduction," she said. "The programs at the time were more prone to victim-blaming and laden with myths like the danger of strangers. They put out tools and strategies that were not effective. Much of the time it was presented as: It's your responsibility to take care of yourself — dress appropriately."

But Flip the Script isn't telling women to behave better. It's showing them how to recognize and react to danger signs in men. Dr. Senn points out that participants are less likely to blame the victim after they take the course. (Both the college health association and Centers for Disease Control and Prevention now recommend Flip the Script.)

"The curriculum talks about how the tendency for women to blame themselves is actually an inhibitor to an effective response," said Sara Feldmann, compliance coordinator in the University of Iowa's office of sexual misconduct. She brought Flip the Script to Iowa, which offers it for credit. "If you're stuck in 'Oh, I didn't communicate clearly' or 'How did I get myself here?' " she said, "it doesn't help you."

"Any kind of a solution that aims its strategies at women makes some people uncomfortable," said Ms. Feldmann. "We don't want to do anything to perpetuate the tendency in our culture to blame victims. If we absolutely knew how to change perpetrator behavior, we would be doing that. But until we figure that out, this is a wonderful program to be able to offer."

TINA ROSENBERG, a former editorial writer for The Times, won a Pulitzer Prize for her book "The Haunted Land: Facing Europe's Ghosts After Communism." She is also the author, most recently, of "Join the Club: How Peer Pressure Can Transform the World" and of the World War II spy story e-book "D for Deception." Ms. Rosenberg is a co-founder of the Solutions Journalism Network, which supports rigorous reporting about responses to social problems.

Making Consent Cool

BY NATALIE KITROEFF | FEB. 7, 2014

IN 1993, when Antioch College introduced its "ask first" policy — mandating that students solicit permission for every intimate advance, including kissing — the policy was widely derided.

Once the stuff of "Saturday Night Live" parody, "consent" today is proudly emblazoned on T-shirts, underwear and condom wrappers.

Through activism that happens as often on YouTube and Twitter as on the main green, foot soldiers in the consent movement are encouraging fellow classmates to ask first and ask often before engaging in sexual activity. Their mission is to make consent cooler than Antioch did. The movement's slogan: "Consent is sexy."

It isn't always an easy sell. Today, as it was decades ago, the butt of the joke is the awkward formality of the ask. Sayda Morales co-founded All Students for Consent at Whitman College in Walla Walla, Wash., last year. She hears from students: "Do I have to ask if I can move one inch closer? Do I have to ask if I can move my left hand one inch on their buttocks?"

But it doesn't have to take on the air of a contract signing, she tells them. When she stands in front of the freshman class, she tries to keep the conversation light. "Consent is necessary," she says, "and it's fun."

Getting consent should be just one part of a frank conversation about what is and isn't O.K. during sex, she says, and can enhance the sexual experience rather than stifle it.

Ms. Morales says she shrugs off student giggles. "At least they're talking about it," she says.

Sometimes it pays to play on the mockery. In 2012, Rebecca Nagle and Hannah Brancato created a website advertising a supposedly new line of Victoria's Secret underwear. True to form, they were frilly, lacy and kaleidoscopic. But instead of "sure thing," the thongs were

GENDER DIVIDE

Men and women don't always agree about what constitutes consent, according to two open-response surveys of 185 heterosexual students last year. The studies, led by Kristen N. Jozkowski of the University of Arkansas, were published in the peer-reviewed Journal of Sex Research.

How men say they get consent

27% Give a directive (*"We are going to have sex."*)

22% Ask if she wants to have sex

14% Use aggressive strategies
(*"I would tell her, let's have sex! Before she could say anything, I would just take off her pants."*)

13% Pretend intercourse occurred by mistake
(*"Start having sex and then say, oops, didn't mean for it to go in, so too late now."*)

When women say they indicate consent

47% Only after being asked by the man
(*"I believe the male should always chase the female."*)

	How women say they give consent	How men interpret a woman's consent
Body language	10%	61%
Verbal cues	50%	9%
Verbal and nonverbal	23%	22%
Just let it happen or not say no	14%	6%

Source: University of Arkansas

THE NEW YORK TIMES

decorated with fiats like "no means no" and "ask first." Before everyone picked up on the prank, the website went viral.

The two activists — through their Baltimore organization, Force: Upsetting Rape Culture — have been at the forefront of a new, edgier tone in consent advocacy. Their group held workshops at 10 colleges last year, educating students on how to spread the anti-rape message. Campus groups are trumpeting their message through "Consent Days," and sometimes weeks, filled with panels, group discussions and consent-branded T-shirt and condom giveaways.

"We are inserting the conversation into culture that people are used to consuming, so that they're able to imagine that this could be a part of that mainstream culture," Ms. Brancato says.

In September, Force pulled a hoax on another brand. Timed to coincide with Playboy's annual list of top party schools, Ms. Nagle and Ms. Brancato created Partywithplayboy.com, which purported to host Playboy's "ultimate guide to a consensual good time." The reasoning for the list, noted the website's cheeky copy, was that "Consent is all about everyone having a good time. Rape is only a good time if you're a rapist."

Stepping Up to Stop Sexual Assault

BY MICHAEL WINERIP | FEB. 7, 2014

BYSTANDER INTERVENTION is so easy to grasp, even by the most inexperienced college freshman, that the program may well be the best hope for reducing sexual assaults on campuses. Mostly it is common sense: If a drunk young man at a party is pawing a drunk young woman, then someone nearby (the bystander) needs to step in (intervene) and get one of them out of there. Of course, that can be tricky at times.

Jane Stapleton, a University of New Hampshire researcher who runs bystander intervention programs at colleges around the country and in Europe, tells students they'll need to be creative about outmaneuvering aggressors. Among the diversions she discusses: suddenly turning on the lights at a party or turning off the music; accidentally spilling a drink on the guy; forming a conga line and pulling him away from the woman he's bothering and onto the dance floor. One of her favorites came from a young woman who approached her drunken girlfriend and said, loudly, "Here's the tampon you asked for."

A definite mood killer, says Ms. Stapleton.

The goal is to stop bad behavior before it crosses the line from drunken partying to sexual assault. "We're definitely not looking to create Captain Bystander here," Ms. Stapleton says. In the best of circumstances, a drunken aggressor won't realize he's been had.

Men as well as women are being called upon to make it work. While the public discussion on sexual violence has primarily focused on the physical and emotional damage done to women, it is also true that getting arrested for sexual assault can mark a young man for life.

Sgt. Richard Cournoyer, a Connecticut state trooper, has investigated a dozen sexual assault cases in the last few years involving University of Connecticut students. "These aren't people jumping out of the bushes," he says. "For the most part, they're boys who had too much to drink and have done something stupid. When we show up to question them, you can see the terror in their eyes."

On Jan. 22, at a White House meeting on sexual violence, President Obama released a report that cited the need for men to intervene: "Bystanders must be taught and emboldened to step in and stop it."

The hope is that bystander programs will have the same impact on campus culture that the designated driver campaign has had in reducing drunken driving deaths (to 9,878 in 2011 from 15,827 in 1991). And that it can be inculcated in a relatively short time; Mothers Against Drunk Driving was founded in 1980 and within a decade was making a difference.

Both take the same tack: Drinking to excess can't be stopped but the collateral damage can.

At a bystander training session for the University of New Hampshire football team last fall, Daniel Rowe, a sophomore, told his teammates that he would use whatever trickery it took to keep them out of trouble.

KATHERINE TAYLOR FOR THE NEW YORK TIMES

A campaign at the University of Massachusetts, Amherst.

"Maybe you don't get the girl," he said, "but you'll keep your scholarship and still be on the team."

He has watched a drunken teammate pressuring a woman at a party and pulled him aside. "I said, 'You know she doesn't want to talk to you, but there's this other girl downstairs who really likes you.' "

There was no girl downstairs.

Sometimes, at a big party, Mr. Rowe won't drink, essentially making himself the designated interventionist.

Lena Ngor, a University of Massachusetts senior, says that at about half a dozen parties a semester she has girlfriends who get drunk and need rescuing. At one party, a guy was all over her friend, so Ms. Ngor put an arm around her and told him, "She's mine, you can't have her." When he suggested a threesome, she declined. "No way you can handle all this," she said.

David E. Sullivan, a district attorney in western Massachusetts, prosecutes about a dozen sex crimes a year at five area campuses, including the University of Massachusetts and Amherst College. He is also the father of three daughters, and it scares him to think that, as numerous researchers have documented, nearly one of five women is sexually assaulted during her college years. "Can you imagine if you told parents there was a one in five chance that their daughter would be hit by a bus? No one would send their kid to college."

With several high-profile rapes roiling campuses and an enforcement push by the Obama administration, public attention has been focused on sexual assault in a way not seen since a generation of feminists first raised these issues in the 1980s. In just the past few months, victims of sexual assault from Amherst College, the University of Connecticut and Vanderbilt have filed federal complaints faulting their schools for inadequate responses.

For everyone involved, says David Lisak, a longtime researcher on campus rape, "It is a murky mess." That includes the young women who are filing complaints, the young men being accused and the outdated campus judicial systems trying to affix innocence or guilt. "All these colleges are struggling independently to figure this out," Mr. Lisak says. "They're all scared."

At last month's meeting on sexual violence, President Obama announced the creation of a task force to coordinate a federal response to campus rape, including ensuring that colleges comply with the law and develop effective policies, and he pledged to offer more support.

Some of the frustration for colleges can be traced to April 2011, when the Department of Education's Office of Civil Rights issued what has come to be known as the "Dear Colleague" letter. It warned that under the 1972 Title IX legislation (until then used primarily to assure parity between men's and women's athletics) colleges were mandated to have a comprehensive system in place for dealing with sexual violence complaints. Failure to do so could result in a university losing tens of millions of dollars in federal funding.

In a few instances the Dear Colleague letter provided specific guidelines; mostly it left universities to figure out how to carry out the mandate. For this reason, Dartmouth is inviting representatives from two dozen universities to meet this summer to begin putting together a system of best practices for campus tribunals.

Many colleges have also responded by developing violence prevention campaigns around the bystander intervention model. Northeastern University's Center for the Study of Sport in Society, which pioneered bystander training 20 years ago, has seen a marked uptick in demand. As Jarrod Chin, its director of training, says, "There is nothing like the threat of losing money to get people's attention."

In the last year, with financial support from District Attorney Sullivan's office, the University of Massachusetts has created an extensive campaign to promote awareness. Posters with messages like "Be a Man, Show Me Respect," "Don't Be a Passive Bystander" and "Do Something" are all over campus, in libraries, locker rooms, even on the sides of buses. All 450 resident assistants have been given bystander training. Several public service videos featuring students, including one narrated by the chancellor, Kumble R. Subbaswamy, are being used as teaching tools. At a midsummer orientation for freshmen, and again the first weekend of school, a university theater group, the Not Ready for Bedtime Players, presented skits about assault and intervention.

Incoming freshmen are the primary target. A study by United Educators, an insurance company owned by more than 1,200 member colleges and universities, found that 63 percent of accusers in sexual assault cases are first-year students.

Enku Gelaye, a vice chancellor overseeing the campaign, says that as with the designated driver, the hope is that by giving the intervention a formal name and linking it to a prescribed set of responses, when something goes wrong a light bulb will go off in students' heads, they will recognize what they are seeing and will remember what to do. "It takes it away from being a fluffy and amorphous idea," she says.

The training may have played a role in catching a rapist on the UMass campus at the start of the fall semester. According to a police report and interviews with prosecutors, at 1:16 a.m. on Labor Day, an 18-year-old freshman stopped a young woman heading home alone from a party. Both had been drinking. He pinned her against a tree and began kissing and biting her neck. "I remember his grip around my neck making it harder to breathe," she told the police. "I was trying to yell but I couldn't because of the way he had his hands." After 10 minutes, she was thrown to the ground, her legs "forced open," her underwear "moved to the side," and raped.

In the midst of this, two groups of students — a total of eight bystanders, a combination of freshmen and juniors, five women and three men — intervened. (While they have not been identified, it is known that the freshman class had attended a presentation on bystander intervention that holiday weekend and that one of the juniors had been a resident assistant.)

According to the report, one witness used her smartphone to take photos of "a male party, which appeared to be naked from the waist down, on top of a female party," while others assisted the woman off the ground and out of the immediate area. After making sure she was safe, they called for help and stayed with her until the police arrived and arrested the man.

Patrick Durocher, 18, has been charged with felony rape. He has pleaded not guilty.

The University of New Hampshire has developed one of the most comprehensive research, training and prevention programs in the country and it was spurred, in part, by an equally brutal campus rape back in 1987 when no one intervened.

According to an account in New England Monthly at the time, an extremely drunk freshman was led into a Stoke Hall dorm room by three drunk sophomores who took turns having sex with her. One went into the hallway and bragged that they had a train going, high-fiving his friends. Several students, including the resident assistant, knew what was going on but did not put an end to it. Nor did the roommate intervene as the three boys tried to pressure the girl into saying it was consensual.

The next morning the woman was too drunk to remember, but a few days later, after piecing it together, she filed a complaint with the university. After four nights of hearings before a campus tribunal at a 170-seat lecture hall that was open to the public, two of the boys were found in violation of a university rule called Respect for Others and were suspended for the fall semester. In criminal court, they pleaded guilty to a misdemeanor and spent two months in jail. The third was cleared.

Women on campus, including Ms. Stapleton, the researcher, led protest marches, occupied a dean's office and at one point surrounded him, linked arms and refused to let him go until he responded to their demands. It took months, but eventually the administration started making the changes that are in place today.

A rape treatment crisis center has been funded and is well staffed; a team of 12 professors and researchers have formed a center for evaluating and implementing bystander programs; and the athletic department holds mandatory sessions for all varsity athletes.

It appears to have had an impact. Shortly after the 1987 rape, 37 percent of female students reported experiencing unwanted intercourse or other sexual contact; by 2006, it was 21 percent, and by 2012, 16 percent.

On most campuses, athletes commit a disproportionate number of sex crimes; the United Educators study found that they make up between 10 and 15 percent of the student population but account for 25 percent of assaults. Not at the University of New Hampshire.

In 2007, the athletic department revamped its public health program, requiring all freshman varsity athletes to take seminars on hazing and bullying; alcohol and drug use; sexual responsibility and consent; and diversity. Last semester, a mandatory session on bystander intervention was added for sophomores. The results are significant. In 2013, seven athletes had cases before the judicial affairs office compared with 75 in 2007.

College men use two words to describe when a man gets in the way of another man's business, and it is not "bystander intervention." For the purposes of a family newspaper, call it "shot blocking."

This was on Matt Martel's mind during a taxi ride home with a friend and a very drunk woman they'd met at a UMass party. "The two of them were touching, cuddling, it was obvious she was down for whatever," says Mr. Martel, a junior. "She'd lost her inhibitions to the point that it really seemed like a good idea for her to go home with this guy she hardly knew."

Mr. Martel got between them to take her back to her dorm. "I said, 'Dude, come on, she's hammered,' " he recalls. His friend was angry. "It was outright awkward," Mr. Martel says. The next day the girl thanked him, but Mr. Martel didn't take a lot of pleasure from it. "I could tell she didn't remember what she was thanking me for," he says, "but someone told her she should, so she did."

More than 60 percent of claims involving sexual violence handled by United Educators from 2005 to 2010 involved young women who were so drunk they had no clear memory of the assault.

College officials have come to realize that campus tribunals are ill-equipped to handle the growing volume of these cases, which often devolve into a he said/she said battle. Honor codes were designed to investigate plagiarism, fighting, alcohol and drug use, not rape. Campus tribunals are made up of students, faculty and administrators. "They're amateurs," says Robb Jones, senior vice president of United Educators.

In the past, colleges have resisted cooperating with local prosecutors for fear of drawing attention to campus crime. But tougher enforcement of federal laws, demanding more transparency, is changing that. For a year now, District Attorney Sullivan's office has been holding monthly meetings with representatives from the University of Massachusetts and other nearby colleges to review sexual assault cases. "Anything that's reported on campuses, we want to see," says Jennifer Suhl, a sex crimes prosecutor in Mr. Sullivan's office. "We don't want them to screen anything out."

A year and a half ago, Xavier University of Ohio resisted cooperating with the local prosecutor and learned a hard lesson.

In July 2012, a female student reported to the campus police that Dez Wells, a star basketball player, had raped her. Mr. Wells acknowledged having sex with the woman but said it was consensual and he used a condom. That night, according to legal papers filed by Mr. Wells, the two plus several friends gathered in a dorm room to play truth or dare. Many of the dares, Mr. Wells said, were sexual — at one point the woman gave him a lap dance; at another, she exposed her breasts. Afterward, they went back to her dorm room and had sex. Several hours later the woman reported to the police that she had been raped.

Joseph T. Deters, the Hamilton County prosecuting attorney based in Cincinnati, says that he put two of his best assistants on the case, including the head of the criminal division. They were convinced no rape had occurred. "It wasn't close," he says. They presented it to a grand jury, which did not indict.

Mr. Deters says he repeatedly tried speaking with Xavier officials, but they did not respond. Instead, the university brought the case before its tribunal.

When Mr. Deters read the transcript of that hearing, he says: "It shocked me. There were students on that conduct board, looking at rape kits; they'd say, 'I don't know what I'm looking at.' "

The tribunal found Mr. Wells "responsible for rape" and expelled him. Soon after, he enrolled at the University of Maryland. The N.C.A.A. requires transfers to sit out a year but made a rare exception in Mr. Wells's case after consulting with Mr. Deters.

"I told them he was a really good kid, he'd never been in trouble with the law and I didn't believe he'd done anything wrong," Mr. Deters says.

Xavier now refers all assault cases to his office.

As for Mr. Wells, several times last season at away games, including one at Duke when he scored 30 points, fans taunted him about being a rapist, shouting, "No means no." He is suing Xavier for his expulsion.

IT IS MOSTLY WOMEN who have spearheaded the fight against sexual assault, founded the rape prevention centers, staffed the hotlines, dominated the research in the field, led the Take Back the Night marches and organized the sexual consent campaigns. And it is men who commit most of the world's violence.

While true, put this way, men feel like the enemy. "What I hear from men," says Ms. Gelaye, the University of Massachusetts vice chancellor, "is they feel like they're the targets, they're the problem."

The fact is, most aren't. Research by Mr. Lisak indicates that about 3 percent of college men account for 90 to 95 percent of rapes. What Ms. Gelaye likes about bystander intervention is that it asks the other 97 percent of men to come into the room and help with the problem.

Jackson Katz, who created the bystander program for men at Northeastern, opened a 2012 Ted Talk by saying sexual assault has been seen as a woman's issue that some good men help out with. "I don't accept that," he said. "I'm going to argue these are men's issues."

Academic research is still in the early stages but is promising. A University of New Hampshire study exposed a group of young men to a bystander intervention campaign like the one at UMass. At the end of several weeks, 38 percent of the men reported having intervened in a sexual assault compared with 12 percent of the group that had not seen the campaign.

At Ohio University, a group of male students took bystander training sessions and were asked four months later if they'd perpetrated a sexual assault; 1.5 percent said they had, compared with 6.7 percent for a control group that had no training.

Enlightened self-interest is a powerful motivator. Several male athletes at a training session last month seemed to feel that bystander intervention was as much about protecting a buddy from getting into trouble as saving a woman from harm.

Andrew Chaput, a member of the U.N.H. soccer team, told a story about getting a text from a friend saying a teammate of his was hanging outside her door and wouldn't leave. "I didn't want him causing trouble, so I took him home," Mr. Chaput said.

The coaches repeatedly pound into their heads that a woman not saying no is not the same as a woman saying yes. "If there is 1 percent doubt in my mind," Mr. Rowe said, "it's not worth doing it. Unless she gives consent, she can say, 'I was raped,' and it's your word against hers."

"If a girl wants to have sex," he continued, "you'll know it. She has that look in her eyes. She's been talking to you, she bothers you, she walks by you all night, the whole thing, you talk, you let it evolve."

Mr. Chaput looked like he had something to say but wasn't sure he should. Finally, in a quiet voice, he said, "I waited until a girl asked me."

Betsy DeVos Reverses Obama-era Policy on Campus Sexual Assault Investigations

BY STEPHANIE SAUL AND KATE TAYLOR | SEPT. 22, 2017

EDUCATION SECRETARY Betsy DeVos on Friday scrapped a key part of government policy on campus sexual assault, saying she was giving colleges more freedom to balance the rights of accused students with the need to crack down on serious misconduct.

The move, which involved rescinding two sets of guidelines several years old, was part of one of the fiercest battles in higher education today, over whether the Obama administration, in trying to get colleges to take sexual assault more seriously, had gone too far and created a system that treated the accused unfairly.

The most controversial portion of the Obama-era guidelines had demanded colleges use the lowest standard of proof, "preponderance of the evidence," in deciding whether a student is responsible for sexual assault, a verdict that can lead to discipline and even expulsion. On Friday, the Education Department said colleges were free to abandon that standard and raise it to a higher standard known as "clear and convincing evidence."

In announcing the change, the latest in a widespread rollback of Obama-era rules by the Trump administration, the department issued a statement saying that the old rules "lacked basic elements of fairness."

The move had been long sought by advocates for accused students, most of whom are men, who had complained that campus judicial processes had become heavily biased in favor of female accusers.

"The campus justice system was and is broken," said Robert Shibley, the executive director of the Foundation for Individual Rights in Education. "With the end of this destructive policy, we finally have the opportunity to get it right."

Education Secretary Betsy DeVos delivering a speech in Washington this week. On Friday she rescinded Obama-era guidelines on campus sexual assault investigations.

Ms. DeVos plans to enact new rules after a public comment period that department officials said could take at least several months, and in the meantime, colleges may choose to maintain the lower standard of proof. She did not provide any hints about whether the final rules would force schools to adopt the higher standard.

Some states followed the lead of the Obama administration and passed laws requiring colleges to use the lower standard. But the move on Friday suggests Ms. DeVos wants colleges to consider making the change if they are legally able, raising the possibility that different colleges will begin to evaluate sexual assault complaints in different ways.

Janet Napolitano, the president of the University of California system and a Homeland Security secretary in the Obama administration, said in a statement that the department's announcement would "in effect weaken sexual violence protections, prompt confusion among campuses about how best to respond to reports of sexual violence and sexual harassment, and unravel the progress that so many schools have made." (California is one of the states now requiring the lower standard.)

And Fatima Goss Graves, president of the National Women's Law Center, an advocacy group for women's rights, said Ms. DeVos's announcement would have a "devastating" impact on students and schools.

"It will discourage students from reporting assaults, create uncertainty for schools on how to follow the law and make campuses less safe," she said in a statement.

Since many cases come down to one student's word against another's, and do not rise to the level of a police investigation, the evidentiary standard has become the main battleground in the nationwide fight over sexual behavior on campus.

The "preponderance" rule means colleges must find a student responsible if it is more likely than not that the student conducted a sexual act without the partner's consent. A "clear and convincing" case means it is highly probable the misconduct occurred.

Even some liberal legal figures took issue with the Obama administration's approach, arguing that no student should be punished unless the school was more certain that a line had been crossed.

Dozens of disciplined students have sued their colleges, some of them successfully, claiming that their rights had been violated.

"The vast majority of campus sexual assault cases involve a lot of alcohol and no witnesses, so you essentially have two people who were probably drinking trying to recall events that may have happened weeks, months, or even years before," said Justin Dillon, a lawyer in Washington who has represented dozens of college men accused of sexual misconduct.

One of his clients sued the Education Department last year, saying he had been found responsible for sexual assault only because the University of Virginia, where he was a law student at the time, had switched to the lower standard. According to his lawsuit, the accuser said that she had been unable to consent to sex because of alcohol consumption, while he claimed the accuser did not even appear to be intoxicated, let alone incapacitated.

There are likely to be other immediate effects of Ms. DeVos's moves.

She eliminated a requirement that investigations be completed in 60 days, now suggesting that the time frame be "reasonably prompt." The department will also allow mediation — sessions in which an accuser and accused hash out their differences — if both sides agree. Mediation was not permitted under the Obama administration guidelines, on the belief that women would feel pressure to participate.

Christina Hoff Sommers, a scholar with the conservative American Enterprise Institute who has written about sexual assault, applauded the administration's decision to permit mediations, saying that some victims were not necessarily seeking a full-blown investigation and a trial. "I think it's misguided to depict the average undergraduate in terms of oppressor and oppressed," she said.

But Cari Simon, a Washington lawyer who represents sexual assault victims, said that colleges could use mediation to avoid addressing serious accusations. "Mediation allows schools to sweep sexual violence under the rug, treating it as a misunderstanding between students," she said.

The Obama administration investigated hundreds of colleges based on student complaints that they had failed to adequately enforce sexual assault regulations. The Education Department had forced a number of colleges to change their procedures by threatening loss of federal funding.

Department officials, in a conference call with reporters on Friday, indicated that they might discontinue some of the 350 or so active investigations if those cases hinged on rules that have now been rescinded.

Those rules — delivered in a 2011 "Dear Colleague" letter sent to colleges by the Obama Administration that laid out how sexual assault complaints were to be handled, as well a 2014 follow-up — came in response to accounts of colleges failing to take complaints seriously,

Betsy DeVos Ends a Campus Witch Hunt

OPINION | BY BRET STEPHENS | SEPT. 8, 2017

SUPPOSE YOU'RE THE KIND of thoughtful liberal who concluded from Donald Trump's election that you've been living in a bubble and need to better understand the causes of America's distemper. Suppose, too, that you have friends who voted for Trump — and who you know for a fact are neither bigots nor buffoons.

Why are they so angry? How could they feel so desperate, politically speaking, to cast their ballots for him?

For a sense of the answer, look no further than Education Secretary Betsy DeVos's announcement Thursday that her department would revisit the Obama administration's Title IX guidelines on campus sexual assault. The guidelines, she said, had "failed too many students" by radically curtailing due process. She's right.

In April 2011, the department's Office of Civil Rights sent a "Dear Colleague" letter to campus administrators effectively demanding new procedures when it came to handling sexual assault cases. The letter arrived without the usual "notice-and-comment" period that is supposed to precede formal rule making. Instead, as Lara Bazelon notes in Politico, "hundreds of schools were placed under federal investigation for failing to be tougher in handling allegations of campus sexual assault."

Campus administrators got the message. Henceforth, the accused would be judged on a "preponderance of evidence" basis to determine guilt, sometimes known as the "50 percent plus a feather" standard. Accusers would be able to appeal "not guilty" verdicts. Efforts would be made to spare the accuser from being faced with direct cross-examination by the accused.

One way to think about the 2011 letter is as an effort to combat the scourge of campus rape. That's a laudable goal, even if evidence of its epidemic proportions is sketchy and good numbers are all but impossible to come by. In 2015, 89 percent of colleges and universities reported zero incidents of rape.

But another way to think about the letter is as Exhibit A in the overreach of an administrative state pursuing a narrow ideological agenda through methods both lawless and aggressive.

Thus, a letter posing as mere "guidance" could acquire the force of holy writ because no campus administrator was going to risk his federal funds for the sake of holding dear the innocence of students accused of rape. A standard of evidence usually applied in civil cases could be used to impose serious sanctions on students for sexual acts of a criminal nature. The Fifth Amendment protection against double jeopardy could be ignored because campus tribunals aren't courts of law. So, too, could the Sixth Amendment right of the accused "to be confronted with the witnesses against him."

This wasn't some theoretical exercise. "After my son received notice that he had been accused of rape I went to the top-tier university he attended and in my first meeting was told he should leave voluntarily because there was no possibility that he could ever be found innocent," one father wrote me. (I omit his name so as not to stigmatize the family.)

His son passed two polygraph exams attesting to his innocence. It made no difference. "I was naïve and thought there was no way this could happen in the United States," the father added. "Now my son is forever marked as having committed a sexual assault."

Kimberly Lau, an attorney at Warshaw Burstein, has represented over 100 defendants in campus sexual-assault cases. She described to me sitting with a client in a campus tribunal where she was forbidden from speaking. The accuser appeared via Skype but did not face the accused.

"They are requiring these 19- or 20-year-old kids to advocate for themselves," she says. "They have to speak about a very private event to three strangers, generally much older. Their whole education is at

A: The essence of affirmative consent is making sure that your partner is totally good about what's happening and there's no reservation. You can make sure in lots of different ways. You don't have to ask at every juncture, "Can I unbutton your blouse?" "Can I touch your breasts?"

If you're really committed to looking for the nonverbal signals, you're just going slowly and making sure from your partner's body language and eye contact that she's clearly into it. If you can't tell, then you stop and ask with words. Once you get the hang of it, it really doesn't need to be that big of a deal. It's just like talking about S.T.I.s or birth control before sex. We've learned how to do that, I hope, without destroying the possibility of eroticism afterwards.

Q: *The campaign is in its infancy, but what's the response been like among men so far?*

A: Some men are saying that they don't need to sign it, because they think it's ridiculous and unnecessary, or because they feel confident they've never, ever violated consent.

Some men get it instantly. I am actively encouraging them to do outreach to other men. I want to build an army of male missionaries of affirmative consent, and these are my guys. Some men agree with it, but they're scared to sign it or talk about it publicly. I can empathize with these men.

I'm a writer who writes openly about sex, drugs and rock 'n' roll, so to speak. I grew up in a political family and am used to a lot of public jostling. But I must admit, even I am scared about talking about these issues right now.

Q: *Was your father an inspiration to you in this campaign?*

A: My father set out some really big shoes for me, and I'm not at all convinced I'm filling them, or ever will. But he was my primary example of how to live life as a man. If you look at my father's two memoirs, an undertone is the intense guilt he felt at being part of two systems —

the nuclear holocaust arsenal he helped build as a war planner, and the Vietnam War — that he came to view as, basically, decent people committing truly evil acts.

His books show the process he went through of extracting himself from these systems and doing what he could to counteract them. This is what I was hearing every night, in seemingly endless lectures at the dinner table, since I was a little boy. So I got the message that, when you see yourself as part of a system that is wrong, you need to extract yourself from it, and do what you can to counteract it.

THIS INTERVIEW HAS BEEN EDITED AND CONDENSED.

CHAPTER 4

The Affirmative Consent Debate

In the search to improve sexual consent laws, universities have landed upon the solution of affirmative consent. First instituted by Antioch College in the nineties, it was later adopted by the state of California and university campuses across the country. Affirmative consent teaches "yes means yes," that consent needs to be explicitly stated for a sexual encounter to proceed. This section explores the debate surrounding the implementation of this policy across the country.

'Yes' Is Better Than 'No'

OPINION | BY MICHAEL KIMMEL AND GLORIA STEINEM | SEPT. 4, 2014

SUPPOSE SOMEONE YOU KNOW slightly arrives at your home, baggage and all, and just barges in and stays overnight. When you protest, the response is, "Well, you didn't say no."

Or imagine that a man breaks into your home while you sleep off a night of drunken revelry, and robs you blind. Did your drinking imply consent?

Until now, this has been the state of affairs in our nation's laws on sexual assault. Invading bodies has been taken less seriously by the law than invading private property, even though body-invasion is far more traumatic. This has remained an unspoken bias of patriarchal law. After all, women were property until very recently. In some countries, they still are.

Even in America, women's human right to make decisions about their own bodies remains controversial, especially when it comes to sex and reproduction.

That's why the recent passage of Senate Bill 967 in California is such a welcome game-changer in understanding and preventing sexual assault. The bill, which passed the Senate unanimously after a 52 to 16 vote in the State Assembly, now awaits Gov. Jerry Brown's signature, which is expected. It would make California the first state to embrace what has become known as the "yes means yes" law, because it alters the standard regarding consent to sexual activity on college campuses. It is the first state response to President Obama's initiative on campus sexual assault, announced earlier this year.

Until this bill, the prevailing standard has been "no means no." If she says no (or, more liberally, indicates any resistance with her body), then the sex is seen as nonconsensual. That is, it's rape. Under such a standard, the enormous gray area between "yes" and "no" is defined residually as "yes": Unless one hears an explicit "no," consent is implied. "Yes means yes" completely redefines that gray area. Silence is not consent; it is the absence of consent. Only an explicit "yes" can be considered consent.

This is, of course, completely logical, and fully consistent with adjudicating other crimes. Nevertheless, it is bound to raise howls of protest from opponents of women's equality and their right to make decisions about their own bodies.

"Yes means yes" has been the law of the land in Canada since 1992, yet the reporting of sexual assault has not skyrocketed with this higher standard.

In the 1990s, there was a similar conversation in this country when Antioch College, long a bastion of innovations in education, also decided that consent to sexual activity required more than just a failure to say no. Verbal consent, the new code of conduct stated, was required for any sexual contact that was not "mutually and simultaneously initiated."

When the so-called Antioch rules were first enacted at that college, the reaction was overwhelmingly negative. The anti-feminist chorus howled in derision at feminist protectionism gone berserk. "Saturday Night Live" parodied it. Charlton Heston added it to a list of examples of campus political correctness gone completely out of control. He told an audience at Harvard in 1999 that "at Antioch College in Ohio, young men seeking intimacy with a coed must get verbal permission at each step of the process from kissing to petting to final copulation — all clearly spelled out in a printed college directive."

While doomsayers lamented that the new rules would destroy the mystery of campus sex, the students took it in stride. Instead of, "Do you want to have sex?" they simply asked, "Do you want to implement the policy?"

Of course some guys on campus were against it, in an honest way. "If I have to ask those questions, I won't get what I want," blurted out one young man to a reporter. Bingo.

But seriously, since when is hearing "yes" a turnoff? Answering "yes" to, "Can I touch you there?" "Would you like me to?" "Will you [fill in blank] me?" seems a turn-on and a confirmation of desire, whatever the sexual identity of the asker and the asked.

Actually, "yes" is perhaps the most erotic word in the English language.

One of literature's most enduring works, James Joyce's "Ulysses," concludes with Molly Bloom's affirmative declaration of desire (considered so erotic, in fact, that it was banned for more than a decade after publication): "and then I asked him with my eyes to ask again yes and then he asked me would I yes to say yes my mountain flower and first I put my arms around him yes and drew him down to me so he could feel my breasts all perfume yes and his heart was going like mad and yes I said yes I will Yes."

"Yes means yes" is clearly saner — and sexier. And that's true for both Leopold and Molly Bloom, as well as the rest of us.

MICHAEL KIMMEL is a professor of sociology and gender studies at Stony Brook University. **GLORIA STEINEM** is a writer, feminist organizer and co-founder of Ms. Magazine and the Women's Media Center.

When Yes Means Yes

EDITORIAL | BY THE NEW YORK TIMES | SEPT. 8, 2014

THE CALIFORNIA LEGISLATURE recently approved a bill that would require colleges receiving state-financed student aid to change the definition of consent in their sexual assault policies, replacing the traditional "no means no" standard with "affirmative consent," known colloquially as "yes means yes." The burden would rest on the student initiating sex to obtain a "yes," rather than on the intended partner to convey a "no." Gov. Jerry Brown has until the end of September to sign the bill, which he should.

Introduced in February, the bill was criticized by some as onerous and intrusive, while others warned that "affirmative consent" would lead to injustice for the accused. The original draft specified that consent should be given "by words or clear, unambiguous actions" and noted that "nonverbal" signs could create misunderstanding. Since — obviously — many consensual sexual encounters are nonverbal, the bill could have dangerously expanded the definition of assault. The offending language was removed, however, and the bill now defines consent more simply as "affirmative, conscious, and voluntary agreement to engage in sexual activity." It need not be spoken.

In its current form, SB-967 is not radical. Its underlying message is that silence does not necessarily equal consent, and that it's better to be certain that sex is desired than to commit assault.

The new standard won't convince young men intent on getting their way — a vast majority of assailants are men — to back down, especially if alcohol is in the picture, as it often is. It could, however, improve how colleges handle accusations. In addition to setting an "affirmative consent" standard, the bill requires California colleges to adopt transparent sexual assault policies, protect confidentiality and establish training programs for officials involved in investigating and adjudicating sexual assault.

Proper training will be crucial as officials get used to the new standard, which requires the accused to account for his actions and explain why he thought he'd received consent. Campus administrators will need to know what questions to ask, manage disputes over whether consent was, in fact, "unambiguous," and recognize false charges.

Sexual assault is rampant on campuses, and colleges have failed to respond adequately. "Yes means yes" won't make these problems disappear. But the new standard is worth trying.

Hooking Up at an Affirmative-Consent Campus? It's Complicated

ESSAY | BY EMILY BAZELON | OCT. 21, 2014

ONE AFTERNOON during Labor Day weekend, a group of 15 or so Yale freshmen met in a classroom where history and French classes would soon be held. As they snacked on pretzels and Skittles, a few volunteered to act out a series of scenarios in which one student asks another out for frozen yogurt. In the first bit of role playing, one student was told to make it clear, in an easygoing way, that he or she wants to go out. The recipient of the invitation was told that he or she also wants to go but has a paper due. "How can you show enthusiasm while still turning down the invitation?" a prompt on a card asked. The answer generally wasn't hard to convey or, for the freshmen watching, to interpret. Most students found that they knew how to demur while keeping the door open for next time.

In the second scenario, the stakes rose. Now the inviter must get the other person to the frozen-yogurt shop. And the invitee does not want to go, although — like most of us — he or she doesn't want to be rude. "How would your character handle this unwanted invitation?" the second card read. The interaction made everyone in the room uncomfortable, as the inviter grew increasingly persistent and the invitee tried to fend the other off.

The intended lesson of this 90-minute workshop was that the line between a request and a demand, welcome interest and unwanted pressure, is usually fairly obvious. "This is the skill set people hammer out as little kids," says Melanie Boyd, an assistant dean of student affairs. She wants students to realize that they know how to recognize agreement, refusal and ambiguity.

The workshop reinforced policies, newly adopted by a growing number of universities, requiring students to make sure they have continuing affirmative consent for every phase of a sexual encounter. The policies, many of which have gone into effect in the last year, were created to help clarify internal university investigations of sexual-assault accusations. In the past, the main question was whether the person (usually a woman) who claimed that she was raped had made it clear that she said no ("No means no"). The new rule shifts the inquiry to whether the student accused of assault got a signal of consent ("Yes means yes"). In California, Gov. Jerry Brown recently signed an affirmative-consent bill, making "yes means yes" the standard at the state's colleges and universities. To continue to receive state funds for student financial aid, California institutions investigating allegations of sexual assault must determine whether both parties gave "affirmative, conscious and voluntary agreement." Lack of resistance and silence no longer constitute proof of consent.

"Yes means yes" is part of a new conversation on campus. When I was a Yale student more than 20 years ago, I remember a few women setting up a microphone, after a Take Back the Night march, to tell stories of what we called date rape. But I don't remember anyone thinking the university would do anything about it. Ten years ago, I wrote about a handful of women who wanted better treatment from Yale, but their complaints seemed isolated and not much came of them. Then beginning around 2011, student activists from across the country started going public. They found one another online, called themselves survivors and demanded that their institutions change. And now everyone is talking about the problem, including President Obama.

The activism has forced not just administrators, faculty members and politicians to reckon with what goes on when students have sex, but also young men on campus. The White House wants them to sign on to a campaign called It's on Us. Fraternities are holding training sessions about preventing sexual assault (as many cope with related investigations and lawsuits). At Yale, students are required to participate in multiple workshops on sexual misconduct. "You can't go on Facebook or Twitter for 10 minutes without seeing a post about these issues," a 19-year-old English major told me.

He was confidently navigating the cultural shift. "Asking, 'Are you O.K. with this?' doesn't have to be uncomfortable," he said. "And in the aftermath, it's huge. You have a more positive memory of having sex with that person, because you don't feel worried."

But most male students expressed some nervousness about accidentally running afoul of consent rules, especially because drinking usually precedes a casual hookup. "It creates a crazy gray area that scares the hell out of everyone," one 21-year-old economics major told me. Some wondered whether training can really prepare you for what is often sex between relative strangers. One freshman woman explained the complicated dynamic by telling me about another freshman-orientation workshop, this one on intimacy. She was startled to hear several men say that they found holding hands more intimate than getting a hand job. The male students I talked with pointed out that holding hands, especially in public, is something you do when you are in a relationship, while a hand job could happen during a hookup. In theory, when it comes to sex, it might make sense to talk about what the other person wants as it's happening. But to do so, you might have to be a little bit tender, a little bit vulnerable. It's hard to have that sort of conversation if there's no intimacy.

"It would be much more gratifying, and in both parties' best interest, for both the girl and guy to be straightforward — 'Hey, I'm willing to do this,' " a 19-year-old male water-polo player said. "And yet the vocabulary for it is not really there." Affirmative-consent policies try to address this by recognizing body language as a form of consent. But to most of the men I talked to, this seemed like an invitation to more ambiguity, not less.

One area where the men were more at ease was "bystander intervention." Universities know that probably the biggest threat to women on campus comes from a small group of serial predators who, research suggests, are responsible for most assaults. Some institutions, like Yale, are training students to watch for warnings signs that someone might be at risk. Sophomores take a workshop in which they watch an

wrong." The initiator, in fact, is responsible for securing consent, but because the other party is intoxicated, it may not be obtainable.

Ms. Santiago, who knew all about the issue, having helped put together university-mandated training in sexual assault prevention for her sorority, jumped out of the interpretive rabbit hole, locked eyes with Mr. Frahme and said: "If guys realize they have to ask and get permission — and I've been asked before, it's not that bad — this could wind up protecting everyone."

It wasn't such a mood kill, she said, when a partner paused and asked: "Do you want to do this. Is it O.K.?"

But Mr. Frahme wasn't buying it — at least not yet.

•

Colleges and universities have been scurrying to amend codes of conduct and refine definitions of consent. One reason for the rush is that the Obama administration, which last year launched the "It's on Us" campaign in an attempt to make campuses safer from sexual violence, has threatened to withhold federal funding from institutions that fail to address problems.

This past year saw a blossoming in the "yes means yes" movement, an about-face on "no means no," which suggests that sex can advance until you hear that "no."

"Silence or lack of resistance, in and of itself, does not demonstrate consent."

An estimated 1,400 institutions of higher education now use some type of affirmative consent definition in their sexual assault policies, according to the National Center for Higher Education Risk Management, a for-profit consulting group. California was the first state to institute standards, last fall, followed by New York. Among states that have introduced affirmative consent bills are New Jersey, New Hampshire and Connecticut.

New York's law standardizes prevention and response policies and procedures relating to sexual assault. The consent definition within it, officials say, is not intended to micromanage students' sex lives but to reorient them on how to approach sex and to put them on notice to take the issue seriously.

So how are students incorporating the code into practice? Are they tucking pens and contracts into back jean pockets alongside breath mints and condoms?

To take the pulse of consent culture, I spoke with several dozen students at the University at Albany. Only a few knew about the standards.

"The policy has changed but nobody knows," said Carol Stenger, a sex educator who directs the university's Advocacy Center for Sexual Violence. The education of roughly 17,000 students, as well as faculty and staff members, on what the decree means mostly falls to Ms. Stenger and Chantelle Cleary, a former sex crimes prosecutor and now the university's Title IX coordinator, responsible for investigating complaints of sexual violence.

Ms. Stenger tries to keep her message simple: "Think of it as borrowing a cellphone. You wouldn't just take it. You'd ask for it first." She's been gathering and creating social scenarios to introduce consent at freshman orientation this summer. Upperclassmen will pose provocative statements, especially related to drinking.

The biggest challenge Ms. Stenger faces, she says, is addressing the alcohol question because men and women think the situation is a wash when both are inebriated. "It makes me crazy," she said. "They ask, 'Am I still a victim?' Yes!"

The hope advanced by many sex educators, including Ms. Stenger, is that seeking and receiving consent will render sex healthier, more gender equitable and maybe even sexier.

But it turns out that men and women are not great verbal communicators when it comes to sex. Both genders are likely to follow what Kristen J. Jozkowski, a sex researcher and assistant professor at the University of Arkansas, characterizes as "traditional sexual scripts," whereby men are the pursuers and women the gatekeepers of sex, trained by society to be reluctant. Studies have found these stereotypes, even in the age of hookup sites like Tinder, to be generally true. Men tend to rely on nonverbal cues in interpreting consent (61 percent say they get consent via body language), but women tend to wait to be asked before signaling consent (only 10 percent say they give consent via body language). No wonder there's so much confusion.

"This discrepancy could potentially lead to miscommunication if men are looking for nonverbal cues and women are waiting to be asked," Dr. Jozkowski explained. Women rarely initiate the discussion because they don't want to come off as being promiscuous, she said. "That's why it's so important to deviate from these old scripts."

What she knows for sure is that educating young people on healthy sexual relationships needs to start much earlier than college. She is optimistic that the new campaigns will change behavior, much as antismoking laws and public service announcements changed views regarding smoking.

•

I approached another table at the Campus Center — three juniors whose fondness for pickup basketball had brought them together as freshmen. None were aware of the consent decree. With some keyword coaching, Malik Alexander found the policy announcement in his old emails and read it aloud. He had his buddies' attention.

Mr. Alexander warmed to the idea: "This sounds like something that should be done by everyone in everyday life anyway. I've always been more of a consensual sort of guy."

Kevin Miranda shook his head. "I think that could be difficult in practice," he said. "Can you at least use body language instead of always having to ask out loud?" Yes. California's definition and the revised language going into effect in the fall in New York are clear on this point. Body language and physical clues (say, a clear nod) would count, but both warn that consent can be revoked at any time.

"When consent is withdrawn or can no longer be given, sexual activity must stop."

One student about to graduate with a degree in science, who asked not to be identified given the intimate nature of her story, had read and absorbed New York's law. She said she had had only one sexual encounter in four years at Albany, with a good friend she had begun dating. She was open to having sex but didn't know what to expect, and it took awhile to realize when her partner became domineering and aggressive that this wasn't how it was supposed to go.

"It wasn't something we'd agreed upon," she said. "It wasn't sexy." She told him to stop, she said, and tried to push him away, and that's when "he covered my mouth with his hand" until he was finished.

She never told anyone, not a friend, not a counselor and not her family.

"They'd never look at me the same again."

Did she think it rose to the level of sexual assault? "Yes it did," she said.

And had she considered filing a complaint with the police or the SUNY authorities? "I don't have that kind of courage," she said, "but I commend all strong women who do."

The new law, she believes, will help change behavior going forward. "Now that it's outlined in black and white," she said, "there's really no excuse for people to be doing what they shouldn't be doing."

•

On a sparkling spring afternoon, on the Academic Podium, an imposing postmodern expanse of fountains, cerulean wading pools and grand colonnades, 50 or so women and a smattering of men marched in the annual Slut Walk, a protest against victim blaming. They wielded signs both optimistic ("Consent Is Sexy") and pointed ("Rape Predated Miniskirts"). The night before, to mark sexual assault month,

"The Vagina Monologues" was onstage and "The Hunting Ground," a haunting documentary about rape culture on campus, was onscreen.

However passionate, the protest was somewhat insular, drawing little attention from those socializing or studying on nearby benches.

I met a boisterous foursome of women, all juniors and all transfer students who had gone through orientation last summer. They had learned about bystander intervention (friends looking out for friends), reporting protocols and campus resources for victims of sexual assault. But they were not aware of consent, the concept.

After hearing a bit about it, Daniela Kelly said, "Not a lot of people are going to follow that."

"That's needed more for hookup culture," said Shanice Stephenson.

"And besides, it would be impossible to monitor," said Chinyere Leigh Richardson. "If they'd asked for our input, maybe we'd be more inclined to try it."

Ms. Kelly recounted a day of partying during spring break in Miami.

"This one guy kept tugging at me and touching and pawing me and he just wouldn't stop," she said.

So what did she do?

"I pretended I was dead."

Like an animal?

"Exactly."

Did it work? She shook her head.

O.K., then, given that story, I asked: Of the 10 men she knew and respected most on campus, how many would benefit from training in sexual consent?

Without a moment's pause, she said, "11."

•

About a month after my sit-down with Mr. Frahme, I checked in with him by phone. Since first hearing about the new policy, he said, he had been practicing consent almost religiously. He now asks for consent once or twice during sexual encounters with women he knows well, and four or five times during more casual or first-time hookups.

"I certainly didn't expect the policy to change my behavior," he said, "but it has."

It's getting to be a little more comfortable, he said. He crafts and poses questions like "You O.K. with this?" "Do you still want to go ahead?" and "Hey, you don't have to do this if you don't want to."

One woman he was having sex with for the first time accused him of being devious in asking for consent. She thought he was using reverse psychology to get her in bed. That wasn't it at all, he said.

"I'm just letting them know I'm not trying to pressure anyone into something they are going to regret."

SANDY KEENAN is a freelance editor and writer in New York.

Regulating Sex

OPINION | BY JUDITH SHULEVITZ | JUNE 27, 2015

THIS IS A STRANGE MOMENT for sex in America. We've detached it from pregnancy, matrimony and, in some circles, romance. At least, we no longer assume that intercourse signals the start of a relationship. But the more casual sex becomes, the more we demand that our institutions and government police the line between what's consensual and what isn't. And we wonder how to define rape. Is it a violent assault or a violation of personal autonomy? Is a person guilty of sexual misconduct if he fails to get a clear "yes" through every step of seduction and consummation?

According to the doctrine of affirmative consent — the "yes means yes" rule — the answer is, well, yes, he is. And though most people think of "yes means yes" as strictly for college students, it is actually poised to become the law of the land.

About a quarter of all states, and the District of Columbia, now say sex isn't legal without positive agreement, although some states undercut that standard by requiring proof of force or resistance as well.

Codes and laws calling for affirmative consent proceed from admirable impulses. (The phrase "yes means yes," by the way, represents a ratcheting-up of "no means no," the previous slogan of the anti-rape movement.) People should have as much right to control their sexuality as they do their body or possessions; just as you wouldn't take a precious object from someone's home without her permission, you shouldn't have sex with someone if he hasn't explicitly said he wants to.

And if one person can think he's hooking up while the other feels she's being raped, it makes sense to have a law that eliminates the possibility of misunderstanding. "You shouldn't be allowed to make the assumption that if you find someone lying on a bed, they're free for sexual pleasure," says Lynn Hecht Schafran, director of a judicial education program at Legal Momentum, a women's legal defense organization.

But criminal law is a very powerful instrument for reshaping sexual mores. Should we really put people in jail for not doing what most people aren't doing? (Or at least, not yet?) It's one thing to teach college students to talk frankly about sex and not to have it without demonstrable pre-coital assent. Colleges are entitled to uphold their own standards of comportment, even if enforcement of that behavior is spotty or indifferent to the rights of the accused. It's another thing to make sex a crime under conditions of poor communication.

Most people just aren't very talkative during the delicate tango that precedes sex, and the re-education required to make them more forthcoming would be a very big project. Nor are people unerringly good at decoding sexual signals. If they were, we wouldn't have romantic comedies. "If there's no social consensus about what the lines are," says Nancy Gertner, a senior lecturer at Harvard Law School and a retired judge, then affirmative consent "has no business being in the criminal law."

Perhaps the most consequential deliberations about affirmative consent are going on right now at the American Law Institute. The more than 4,000 law professors, judges and lawyers who belong to this prestigious legal association — membership is by invitation only — try to untangle the legal knots of our time. They do this in part by drafting and discussing model statutes. Once the group approves these exercises, they hold so much sway that Congress and states sometimes vote them into law, in whole or in part. For the past three years, the law institute has been thinking about how to update the penal code for sexual assault, which was last revised in 1962. When its suggestions circulated in the weeks before the institute's annual meeting in May, some highly instructive hell broke loose.

In a memo that has now been signed by about 70 institute members and advisers, including Judge Gertner, readers have been asked to consider the following scenario: "Person A and Person B are on a date and walking down the street. Person A, feeling romantically and sexually attracted, timidly reaches out to hold B's hand and feels a thrill published in the past 20 years, "Unwanted Sex: The Culture of Intimidation and the Failure of Law," he stresses that the draft should be seen as just that — notes from a conversation in progress, not a finished document.

But the case for affirmative consent is "compelling," he says. Mr. Schulhofer has argued that being raped is much worse than having to endure that awkward moment when one stops to confirm that one's partner is happy to continue. Silence or inertia, often interpreted as agreement, may actually reflect confusion, drunkenness or "frozen fright," a documented physiological response in which a person under sexual threat is paralyzed by terror. To critics who object that millions of people are having sex without getting unqualified assent and aren't likely to change their ways, he'd reply that millions of people drive 65 miles per hour despite a 55-mile-per-hour speed limit, but the law still saves lives. As long as "people know what the rules of the road are," he says, "the overwhelming majority will comply with them."

He understands that the law will have to bring a light touch to the refashioning of sexual norms, which is why the current draft of the model code suggests classifying penetration without consent as a misdemeanor, a much lesser crime than a felony.

This may all sound reasonable, but even a misdemeanor conviction goes on the record as a sexual offense and can lead to registration. An affirmative consent standard also shifts the burden of proof from the accuser to the accused, which represents a real departure from the traditions of criminal law in the United States. Affirmative consent effectively means that the accused has to show that he got the go-ahead, even if, technically, it's still up to the prosecutor to prove beyond a reasonable doubt that he didn't, or that he made a unreasonable mistake about what his partner was telling him. As Judge Gertner pointed out to me, if the law requires a "no," then the jury will likely perceive any uncertainty about that "no" as a weakness in the prosecution's case and not convict. But if the law requires a "yes," then ambiguity will bolster the prosecutor's argument: The guy didn't get unequivocal consent, therefore he must be guilty of rape.

So far, no one seems sure how affirmative consent will play out in the courts. According to my informal survey of American law professors, prosecutors and public defenders, very few cases relying exclusively on the absence of consent have come up for appeal, which is why they are not showing up in the case books. There may be many reasons for this. The main one is probably that most sexual assault cases — actually, most felony cases — end in plea bargains, rather than trials. But prosecutors may also not be bringing lack-of-consent cases because they don't trust juries to find a person guilty of a sex crime based on a definition that may seem, to them, to defy common sense.

"It's an unworkable standard," says the Harvard law professor Jeannie C. Suk. "It's only workable if we assume it's not going to be enforced, by and large." But that's worrisome too. Selectively enforced laws have a nasty history of being used to harass people deemed to be undesirable, because of their politics, race or other reasons.

Nonetheless, it's probably just a matter of time before "yes means yes" becomes the law in most states. Ms. Suk told me that she and her colleagues have noticed a generational divide between them and their students. As undergraduates, they're learning affirmative consent in their mandatory sexual-respect training sessions, and they come to "believe that this really is the best way to define consent, as positive agreement," she says. When they graduate and enter the legal profession, they'll probably reshape the law to reflect that belief.

Sex may become safer for some, but it will be a whole lot more anxiety-producing for others.

JUDITH SHULEVITZ is the author of "The Sabbath World: Glimpses of a Different Order of Time" and a contributing opinion writer.

president was the education reformer and politician Horace Mann; Coretta Scott King is among the famous graduates.

But students regularly venture outside this cocoon. Antioch's "cooperative educational experiences" are a cornerstone of the curriculum here, and they compel students, at least four times before graduating, to go on "co-op," taking on 10-week jobs and internships, usually in places far from Yellow Springs, often arranged or provided by Antioch alumni.

If you choose to permeate the bubble yourself and visit Antioch, you will be asked to sign a "statement of understanding" that you will abide by a policy that requires enthusiastic verbal consent during every stage of every sexual interaction. (Reporters are also required to sign the statement.)

Antioch was founded in 1850 but was closed by an umbrella organization in 2008, in part because of financial issues. Alumni worked to gain the college's independence and reopened in 2011. When it did, it guaranteed free tuition to its first four enrolling classes.

Students including Marcell Vanarsdale, 22 and now a fourth-year student, arrived at Antioch mostly unaware of the college's consent policy. "I think my parents raised me pretty well and taught me respect for people and respect for women, but learning about the S.O.P.P. is definitely the first formal education about consent I ever got," said Mr. Vanarsdale, who grew up just outside of Chicago and is studying history and performance.

He attended several sessions at orientation devoted to the policy, including one led by Planned Parenthood educators, another about the history of sexual relations. "It was different, for sure," he said. "The biggest pull was moving away from the idea that 'no means no' and toward 'yes means yes.' "

In its most updated form, the S.O.P.P. is an eight-page document that spells out the tenets of "affirmative consent." In each stage of a sexual interaction, consent must be verbally requested and verbally given, the policy says — and "silence conveys a lack of affirmative consent."

It prohibits the sending of unsolicited sexual text messages and requires partners to disclose sexually transmitted infections. It also dictates that people under the influence of drugs and alcohol cannot give consent. So, strictly speaking, any drunk hookup would be found to be in violation of the policy if one of the parties filed a complaint.

"The S.O.P.P. is Antioch College's formal attempt at ending sexual violence and sexual harassment while fostering a campus culture of positive, consensual sexuality," it reads.

When the policy was enacted in the early 1990s, it became the subject of a lot of media attention, including a blistering skit on "Saturday Night Live" in 1993 starring Shannen Doherty ("major in Victimization Studies") and Chris Farley ("charged in three hazing deaths") as Antioch students competing in a game show hosted by Phil Hartman called "Is It Date Rape?" (The "Jeopardy!"-like categories included "I Paid for Dinner" and "Halter Top.")

Before a national audience, the school and the women who created the policy were portrayed as endemic of a politically correct culture run amok that was trying to desexualize sex.

The reality may be quite the opposite. Antioch recently extended its Sex Week into a month. "We wanted to bring even more pleasure-based sex education and gender-based education," said Iris Olson, a 2017 graduate, who is studying for a master's degree in public health at Boston University and uses the pronouns they/them/their. Mx. Olson, 23, who prefers that gender-neutral honorific, helped organize Month of Sex events.

During them, programming has included screenings of ethical pornography, a "Kiss and Tell" story-sharing event, "Dildo Bingo," a ropes-and-bondage workshop and an Antioch traditional event that students attend dressed to express themselves along the gender continuum.

A "sex positive" culture has everything to do with the S.O.P.P., Mx. Olson said. "Being able to talk to a partner or multiple partners about what you like, what you would like to experiment with — to have a negotiation whether it's about B.D.S.M. or extra cuddling, whatever

A policy for sexual consent introduced in 1990 continues to influence campus culture.

gets you going — those discussions are what make sex wonderful. You have more control of the situation."

The college's administration sees this all as a big selling point for the school. "Our students and our alumni have always been very involved with activism, and social justice is in our DNA," said Mila Cooper, Antioch's vice president for diversity and inclusion and the director of the Coretta Scott King Center. "There's a heightened awareness of sexual violence and sexual assault right now with the MeToo movement, but I do think Antioch has been involved in these conversations long before. It's not just a policy, you know, it's part of the education and the culture here."

'WE LIVE IN A CULTURE WHERE SO MANY ARE PENETRATED PHYSICALLY, EMOTIONALLY AND VERBALLY'

"We talk about taking up space in a lot of different ways," said Toni Jonas-Silver, 23 and a fourth-year student, while sipping tea at the Emporium, a coffee bar and wine shop that is something of an off-campus commissary during the day. "Even in these conversations in class, some people have the tendency to talk so much that it diminishes the chance that other voices will be heard. It's related to people who have more privilege and are more used to being encouraged to take up that space."

The discussions connect back, sometimes directly, to the policy. "The S.O.P.P. is a reminder of who we are and what we're here to do," said Michelle De León, 23, a second-year student. "It lets us say, 'Hey, you're in a community and you're in a space with other people and be mindful of the space you're taking up.' Women, nonbinary people, queer people, people of color — we're not living in a culture that gives them space. We live in a culture where so many are penetrated physically, emotionally and verbally by anyone at any moment."

In the media, it's been misunderstood, many Antiochians say. "People think it's a harsh policy," Ms. Nalubega said. "But it's not. It's saying that when you do touch a person, your touch is exciting and welcoming to that person."

"There's an idea that it has to be very unromantic and very contractual and that's not true at all," said Jeanne Kay, who was an Antioch student and now is working for the school's fund-raising division as the annual giving manager. "You can learn to ask in ways that are sexy and romantic and say, 'Is this O.K.? You want to continue to do this? Can I touch you there?' These are all thing that can enhance the experience instead of killing the buzz."

Still, there is a learning curve. Ms. Navarrette, for one, was not used to having honest conversations about sex. "It can be especially difficult for people of color who are from cultures where women and girls are not supposed to talk about sex," she said. "It means you're a 'bad girl.' "

Many students have come to embrace it as a good thing. "At first, it feels almost unnatural and abrupt to say, 'Hey, can I do this? Can I proceed with this?' " Mr. Vanarsdale said. "But then, you see, at least for me, it's not just what you say but how you say it, getting more comfortable with the language. And I think it takes out a lot of the pressure on both parties when asking is involved and clarity is confirmed."

Enforcement controls how effective a policy can be. The tiny size of the student body is one impediment to ideal outcomes, students say. News of an S.O.P.P. violation being reported to a student community representative or a member of the staff or faculty spreads very quickly. It's pretty much guaranteed that the person reporting the violation will share mutual friends with the person they're citing. This can create a real strain on student social dynamics.

There is also a sense that the administration does not always respond as students think it should. "From the time the school reopened to two summers ago, there were about eight to 10 S.O.P.P. cases," said Malka Berro, a 21-year-old fourth-year student. "Two had administration repercussions. Our perception is that sometimes people don't follow through."

But the reality is sometimes more complicated. Roger D. Stoppa, the director of public safety at Antioch, said that because a reported violation of the S.O.P.P. is, by definition, an unwanted act in the context of a sexual interaction, it must also be considered a violation of Title IX, the federal law that forbids sex discrimination within any entity that receives federal funding.

And federal guidelines prohibit officials from revealing private details of an investigation. "We're sworn to confidentiality. We can't say that we found somebody responsible, and this is the consequence that they got," said Mr. Stoppa, who is also the school's deputy Title IX coordinator. "When they don't see anything tangible happen, they just think, 'Oh my God, I reported and nobody did anything about it.' Well, we go through a very thorough process."

So the student community may ultimately take matters of enforcement into its own hands.

In the summer of 2017, a student group organized a concert

featuring several local bands, that would take place at the on-campus amphitheater. Nonstudents from beyond Yellow Springs attended. They were asked to sign the document stating that they understood and would respect the S.O.P.P. Several of the men refused to sign; they were approached by students who asked them to sign the document or to leave. They left.

"There is a stigma to not signing," Ms. Berro said.

In late 2014, Todd Sanders, now 26, was called to meet with a dean because two S.O.P.P. violations had been filed against him. "I had gotten very active in my romantic life when I was at Antioch," said Mx. Sanders, who is gender-fluid and uses they/them/their pronouns. "I was having difficulty managing being polyamorous. Alcohol became a factor."

The dean read a list of complaints, Mx. Sanders said. Some of them came as a surprise, but not all. Mx. Sanders said they and the dean decided they should leave school.

Mx. Sanders left Yellow Springs for a while but then returned, moved into an apartment in town and got a job at a restaurant. At another meeting, the dean told Mx. Sanders that they were banned from campus, Mx. Sanders said. The rules were not always closely observed. "I remember once I was walking with a few people, we stopped right at the edge of campus, and someone saw me and got really mad at me," they said.

Word of Mx. Sanders's behavior had spread around campus. At first, some students weren't sure how to react because Mx. Sanders was well regarded as an activist.

"At Antioch, we focus so much on inclusion and creating space for marginalized people on campus that I think what has formed is a hierarchy based off of marginalization," Mr. Vanarsdale said. "It gives people who have this marginalization attached to their identity some form of power. Todd wasn't the archetype of what we think toxic masculinity would look like. He wasn't a heterosexual cis male."

Antiochians take their culture of consent seriously, and students were disturbed to know someone living in their midst was not living by the S.O.P.P. Students began to approach Mx. Sanders, asking for apologies or acknowledgments that the consent rules were being flouted. Mx. Sanders didn't seem to be chastened.

In a manner that perhaps can only take place when an entire community buys into a culture of consent, the community took action.

"There was a meeting of people who have been friends with this person or who had sex with this person or who are the victims, and we all got together and decided we had to do something about it," Ms. Nalubega said. "So when we would see him at Birch or at the Emporium or at a party, we would say to him, 'You can't be in this space.'"

By the spring of 2015, it had become more difficult to live in Yellow Springs, Mx. Sanders said. "There was a posting on a student Facebook page saying I was a rapist and people should avoid me. That was a difficult thing to read. Within a month, I left. I felt like I had been run out of town on a rail."

Contemporaries of Mx. Sanders said they tried to compel Mx. Sanders to acknowledge their missteps. "This is someone who was repeatedly confronted and didn't change their behavior and then was ultimately not tolerated in the community," said someone who knew Mx. Sanders but did not want to speak publicly about the matter.

Mx. Sanders is now committed to seeking affirmative consent in sexual interactions. "I don't blame anyone else," Mx. Sanders said. "I need to be accountable."

TAKING IT TO THE NEXT LEVEL

In the fall of 1990, an Antioch student reported a date rape to the dean's office. The administration promised her that the male student would be removed from the dorm in which they both lived. When he was not removed, a group came together at the Womyn's Center to plot for change.

One of the women activists was April Wolford, now in information technology services at the University of California, Berkeley. She was an elected representative to a community council. She thought it was important to codify the demands — to create a policy for the administration to formally adopt.

"The first version we wrote was very punitive," Ms. Wolford said. It was called the "Antioch College Sexual Offense Policy," and it began: "A sexual offense, as defined herein, committed by a community member will not be tolerated by the Antioch community. If there is reasonable cause to believe that any person has committed such an offense and that person is considered a threat to the community, that individual must be promptly removed from the campus."

Sexual offenses were defined as forced physical penetration, "any non-consensual physical contact found to be sexually threatening or offensive" and other incidents of "persistent sexual harassment."

"But what we learned from that is that wasn't the focus of what the community wanted," Ms. Wolford said. "We wanted to prevent these assaults. As young people, we didn't have the tools."

So they began to discuss consent. "The challenge was, 'How do you get consent in a situation where everyone is so nervous?' " Ms. Wolford said.

So the students created not just a policy but an educational curriculum of lectures, discussion groups, presentations from Planned Parenthood and skits in which actors would work through different scenarios where consent should be taught. "It was so owned by students, it was created by students, and students created education around it," Ms. Wolford said. The school administration adopted the policy with enthusiasm in the winter of 1991.

When Louise Smith, a professor of performance who graduated in the class of 1977, first came back to Yellow Springs to join the faculty, the S.O.P.P. was newly in place but already "a prominent part of the zeitgeist," she said. Ms. Smith had come back to Antioch from New York City, where she was entrenched in the downtown performance scene. She thought the policy was too based in political correctness. "I was an eye roller," she said.

But over the years — including a stint as dean of community life in 2011, during which she worked with students to remove S.O.P.P. language about "rape culture" in favor of "sexual violence," which she hoped would be less alienating and accusatory toward men — she has changed her mind.

"I have very little patience with the notion that something like this isn't needed," she said. "I don't feel the policy was meant to stop us from shaking hands without consent. What it does do is sort of say, 'Your body is your body and if you don't want something to happen to it or with it, it shouldn't.' And then that can be applied into every social interaction."

Andy Janecko, 19 and a second-year student, wants to create another policy. "I'm really wanting to write a separate policy, that brings consciousness about consent a little bit further," said Mx. Janecko, who uses they/them/their pronouns. "We're missing this whole component of consent in general, teaching people not to touch people at all if you don't have their verbal consent," they said, suggesting that it could be called the Nonconsensual Contact Prevention Policy.

One reason for the policy, they said, is to protect against people casually touching people who don't like to be touched or who have disabilities that make unexpected touch painful or unsettling.

"I'm also looking for it to help people get justice or get acknowledgments at least for microaggression," said Mx. Janecko, currently on co-op in San Francisco, working at a mime theater. They hope to get to work on this next evolution when they return to campus this spring.

CHAPTER 5

Key Cases

There have been a number of cases that have crystallized the concerns around consent and challenged conventional understandings of what yes and no mean. From Emma Sulkowicz's work of performance art to the debate over Brock Turner's probation sentence, the articles in this section show the cases that have captured national attention and the paths through which the interests of the parties were and were not resolved.

In Florida Student Assaults, an Added Burden on Accusers

BY RICHARD PÉREZ-PEÑA AND WALT BOGDANICH | SEPT. 14, 2014

AFTER DOWNING a double dose of NyQuil to fight a cold, the young woman woke in a man's dormitory room with a vague memory of someone being on top of her, but no recollection of sexual contact. Three days later she found a condom in her vagina. She repeatedly confronted the man, who insisted that nothing had happened, and his roommate, who had told her he saw them having sex, then said he was joking.

"I was worried, and I was crying," the woman, a Florida State University student, told the police. She went to Tallahassee Memorial Healthcare for an examination, and to the university police, but they did not question the suspect or his roommate. Instead, they asked the woman if she wanted the suspect questioned; she never gave a "yes" or "no" answer, so they closed the case 18 days after her initial report.

Last year, the Tallahassee police's handling of a rape accusation against Florida State's famed quarterback, Jameis Winston, who denied the allegation, drew attention to the department's failure to adequately investigate despite bruises on the accuser and semen on her underwear.

Now an examination of other cases from recent years shows a pattern to the handling of sexual assault complaints by Florida State students: After an accuser makes a police report and submits to a medical rape exam, the police ask if she wants them to investigate, and if she does not explicitly agree, they drop the case, often calling her uncooperative.

The pattern emerges from interviews with prosecutors and victims' advocates, and a review of case files obtained by The New York Times from both the Tallahassee police and the university police, under the state's Freedom of Information Law.

The records provide a look at police practices not just locally, but also nationally. Experts say that what happens in Tallahassee is common, although police forces are being encouraged to alter their habits.

"There are a lot of jurisdictions that are trying to do it better, but it's still incredibly common that the police just do not do the investigation," said Rebecca Campbell, a psychology professor at Michigan State University who researches law enforcement treatment of sexual assaults. "They do not treat other crimes this way. If you have a property crime, they don't say: 'Would you like me to dust for fingerprints? Would you like me to canvass the area for witnesses?' "

After getting the accuser's statement, Dr. Campbell said, the police should "do what you would do with any other crime — you investigate, and you go try to catch the bad guy."

That has been the practice in Philadelphia for a few years, said Kathleen M. Brown, an associate professor of nursing at the University of Pennsylvania, who worked with the city police on revising their approach. When a rape exam is done, she said, a victim decides whether to give the evidence to the police and talk with an officer; if she does, the police explain the next steps and assure her that she can stop cooperating at any time, but they do not ask her if they should continue to investigate.

"Agreeing to report is not the same thing as saying, 'I'll get up on the stand and testify,' and that conversation shouldn't happen until much later, if it happens at all," Dr. Brown said. Historically, many officers disbelieved the accusers or wanted to avoid hard-to-prove cases, and discouraged women from reporting rapes, she said, "so we've worked hard to get to this point."

It is unknown how many Florida State University students report sexual assaults to the police. Most occur off campus and are reported to the Tallahassee Police Department, which does not tally which accusers are students, nor does the state attorney's office. Sixteen on-campus rapes were reported to the Florida State University police from 2011 through 2013, but those include nonstudent victims and exclude sex crimes other than rape.

But records from Refuge House, a Tallahassee nonprofit group, obtained as part of an examination of the Winston case, show that in those three years, its nurses were called to hospitals to examine and counsel 63 Florida State students seeking treatment for sexual assault. Of those, 55 reported the assault to the police.

Interviews with prosecutors and a review of local news reports turned up just two arrests in that span by the Tallahassee police for sexual assaults on Florida State students. University police records show no arrests for forcible sex offenses from 2007 through 2013. Unlike burglary, sex is often consensual, so proving rape is hard; in some cases, prosecutors agreed with the police that the evidence did not support charging the suspect.

It is widely accepted that if a victim is adamant that she does not want a case pursued, law enforcement should take that into account. But reports from both city and university police departments show that unless accusers say firmly that they want cases investigated and prosecuted, officers have called them uncooperative and called off investigations.

"I was raped and stressed and scared," one student later wrote in a complaint to the Tallahassee police, "something completely different than not cooperating."

The student who accused Mr. Winston of raping her in December 2012 complained that a police report falsely stated that she had not cooperated and did not want the case pursued. Prosecutors did not learn of the case until months later, and concluded they could not successfully prosecute, but leveled withering criticism at the Tallahassee police for doing little to investigate.

In talking with the police, "they indicate that this happens all the time, victims come in, they're not sure what they want to do, and the case is not investigated until they make up their mind," said Georgia Cappleman, the chief assistant state attorney for a six-county region of Florida that includes Tallahassee.

"If a victim comes in and reports a violent crime, I don't think it's appropriate to then say, 'Well, what do you want to do about it? Are you sure you want to go forward with this?' " Ms. Cappleman said. "The appropriate thing to do is to assume by her being there, making the report, that she does want an investigation and to proceed with it accordingly."

The Tallahassee police did not respond to requests for comment.

In a written statement, the university said its officers are trained to treat people compassionately, including "making sure the alleged victim is aware of, and can prepare for, the next steps." It added that experts counsel that "it is important to allow a victim to have a voice in the investigative process as a way of re-establishing control over their lives."

In the case of the woman who found a condom inside her, the university said, the investigator "respected the desires of the alleged victim," and could reopen the case if she requested it.

Since the Winston case burst into view last year, the Tallahassee police have gotten a new chief, and both that department and the university police have stepped up efforts to train officers in dealing with sexual assault victims, though it is not clear how much day-to-day practice has changed.

In a case from April 2013, the day after a woman went to a hospital and told the Tallahassee police that she had been raped, she told them that she was unsure about prosecuting. When she remained uncertain 17 days later, an officer wrote that she was "unwilling to cooperate with the investigation or proceed with criminal charges" and closed the case. The suspect was not interviewed.

In another case, a student and her family complained repeatedly about the Tallahassee police's treatment of her rape allegation last October. They said officers had treated her more skeptically than the suspect, and one asked if she was sure it was rape and advised her not to tell her father.

The woman had bruises on her neck and inner thigh, she said she had told police that she had fought, and an investigator's report said, "When the victim tried to get up, he would push her down by the neck." Yet the same report said she had not resisted. On the day of the episode, she gave separate interviews to two officers, went to a hospital for an examination and filled out a written statement, but the report referred to her as being "unwillingness to cooperate" when she did not give a follow-up interview later that day.

The department did not make an arrest in the case. It sent the woman a letter saying that it would not formally investigate her complaints, but that one officer "was counseled on how his actions or what he said could be perceived by other people."

Sexual assault cases are notoriously hard to prove in court, and in Leon County, only about one in five police complaints — including those in which no "rape kit" is collected — leads to prosecution. The rate appears to be significantly lower for college students, but it is unclear whether the difference reflects the prevalence of alcohol in college cases, a different approach by the police or other factors.

"I think that's an extremely important question, and we don't have an answer," said Meg Baldwin, executive director of Refuge House.

But, she added, "a factor I would suggest is the social isolation of student victims." Students are away from their homes and support networks, they often report that their college friends shun them for accusing fellow students, and many move back home after an attack, making investigation harder, she said.

When officers ask an accuser if she wants a case to go forward, putting the onus on her to decide, there is a risk "that in the guise of seeking the victim's consent to the investigation, she's actually being bullied out of it," Ms. Baldwin said. "Particularly in the few days after an attack, a victim is very likely to place the interpretation on those kinds of questions as questioning the reliability of her report."

In fact, victims often say they feel doubted by the police, who focus on their behavior and on holes and inconsistencies in their stories. Experts say investigators need to understand that fragmented, even contradictory memories, and unexpected emotional responses, are normal products of trauma.

Sexual assault is the hardest crime to measure because, according to many surveys, most victims never go to the police. An increase in cases can reflect better reporting, not a crime wave. Crime statistics reported by colleges and universities are doubly problematic, because they generally exclude off-campus attacks.

In April, a White House task force on college sexual assault listed as its first recommendation that every college conduct a campus climate survey, to try to gauge the extent of the problem.

In a Mattress, a Lever for Art and Political Protest

BY ROBERTA SMITH | SEPT. 21, 2014

Editor's Note: The language of this article has been updated to reflect Emma Sulkowicz's use of nonbinary honorifics and pronouns.

YOU CAN, for the moment, call Emma Sulkowicz a typically messianic artist, and they won't object. I used the phrase, sitting in their tiny studio at Columbia University on Thursday, as we discussed "Carry That Weight." This is the succinct and powerful performance piece that is their senior art thesis as well as their protest against sexual assault on campus, especially the one they say they endured.

"Carry That Weight," which is beginning its fourth week, involves Mx. Sulkowicz carrying a 50-pound mattress wherever they go on campus (but not off campus). Analogies to the Stations of the Cross may come to mind, especially when friends or strangers spontaneously step forward and help them carry their burden, which is both actual and symbolic. Of course another analogy is to Hester Prynne and her scarlet letter, albeit an extra heavy version that Mx. Sulkowicz has taken up by choice, to call attention to their plight and the plight of others who feel university officials have failed to deter or adequately punish such assaults. The carried mattress also implies disruption and uprootedness, which call to mind refugees or homeless people.

The subject of sexual assault on campuses surfaced on the national stage on Friday, when President Obama and Vice President Joseph R. Biden Jr. announced the formation of It's On Us, a national campaign on this issue. They addressed it in blunt and unequivocal terms. "Society still does not sufficiently value women," the president said.

Mx. Sulkowicz spoke of their interest in the kind of art that elicits a powerful response, whether negative or positive. Freshly painted on the walls around us loomed big black letters spelling out the "rules of engagement," the guidelines to their performance: One states that they

Emma Sulkowicz, left, and Gabriela Pelsinger carry a mattress on the Columbia University campus as part of Mx. Sulkowicz's performance piece "Carry That Weight."

will continue the piece until the man they accuse of attacking them is no longer on campus, whether he leaves or is expelled or graduates, as they also will next spring. (If need be, they plan to attend commencement carrying the mattress.) They said the performance is giving them new muscles and an inner strength they didn't know they had, and is attracting many different kinds of attention, some of it hard to take.

"Carry That Weight" is both singular and representative of a time of strongly held opinions and objections and righteous anger on all sides, a time when, not surprisingly, political protest and performance art are intersecting in increasingly adamant ways.

You can see this merging in the Guy Fawkes masks worn by members of Anonymous, a loose international network of hactivists, at protests against, for example, the Church of Scientology or the killing of Michael Brown in Ferguson, Mo. You can also see it in some of the performance-like protests that greeted the opening this month of the David H. Koch

Plaza at the Metropolitan Museum of Art or those that were carried out last spring in the rotunda of the Guggenheim Museum to call attention to the general plight of laborers in the United Arab Emirates who are expected to build its latest outpost there. There are numerous other instances: Protests in London in 2011 against the Tate's accepting sponsorship from BP included a performer splashed with oil, lying naked on the floor of the great hall of Tate Britain like a bird caught in an oil spill.

Mx. Sulkowicz's effort is somewhere near this intersection, but not at its center. Combining aspects of endurance, body and protest art and participatory relational aesthetics, it is a highly specific work of art in its own right, carefully conceived and carried out by one person expending considerable thought, time and energy for a very long time (up to eight months). It comes from a history that includes the relatively solitary ordeals of Vito Acconci, Tehching Hsieh and Marina Abramovic, but also relates tangentially to more extreme physical

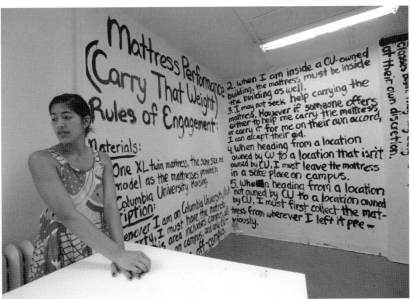

Emma Sulkowicz, a Columbia senior, in their art studio. On the walls are rules for their performance piece, a protest against the university's handling of their charges of sexual assault on campus.

acts of political resistance — the fasts of jailed suffragists in early-20th-century Britain come to mind.

"Carry That Weight" might be called an artwork of last resort. It is the culmination of two years of pain, humiliation, frustration and righteous anger that began in 2012. On the evening of the first day of classes of their sophomore year, Mx. Sulkowicz said, they were anally raped in their dorm room by a fellow student with whom they had had consensual sex twice before, according to the police report.

In the aftermath, Mx. Sulkowicz suffered in silence, then filed a complaint with the university. This led to a hearing before a panel that found him not responsible, according to a campus newspaper report in The Columbia Spectator, a decision that was upheld upon appeal. After that disappointment, they said, a trip last May to file a report with the police was so upsetting Mx. Sulkowicz didn't follow through, although they secretly recorded it on their cellphone.

The performance piece began to take shape in Mx. Sulkowicz's mind during a residency at Yale Summer School of Art and Music in Norfolk, Conn., this past summer. First they made a short video that showed them dismantling a bed, with the police station tape as audio. But soon they focused on the mattress alone and using it on campus, with the simplest, most public action being to carry it. The foam mattress and its dark blue cover are identical to the standard issue one on which they said the rape occurred and were not easy to track down and purchase; the rules of engagement similarly took a lot of refinement and every day still present them with new logistical problems to work out. (For example, going to the subway requires walking a few extra blocks since they can't cut across campus without the mattress.)

One of the most effective aspects of the piece is the way it fluctuates between private and public, and solitary and participatory. They said they rarely walk very far without someone lending a hand and entering into what Mx. Sulkowicz calls "the space of performance." Indeed, shortly after leaving their studio on Thursday afternoon, they ran into their best friend, Gabriela Pelsinger, who took over one end of the mattress, in effect becoming one of the performers. (One of the rules is that Mx. Sulkowicz cannot ask for help, but they can accept it.)

Ms. Pelsinger, like Mx. Sulkowicz, is among a group of more than 20 people who have joined in a Title IX complaint with the federal government's Department of Education against Columbia, charging that it mishandled their individual gender-based misconduct or sexual assault cases.

Suzanne B. Goldberg, special adviser to the university's president, Lee Bollinger, on sexual assault prevention and response, and director of Columbia Law School's Center for Gender & Sexuality Law, said in a statement, "As the university has made clear in many different ways during the past month, major steps have been taken to enhance the gender-based misconduct policy and resources available to all Columbia University students." Ms. Goldberg said the university does not comment on individual cases. She added, "The university embraces the attention that students and others have brought to the issue."

As Mx. Sulkowicz and Ms. Pelsinger proceeded across campus, some people smiled while others looked puzzled. There were comments. "There they go again," one woman said to her companion as they walked past me. Midway through the journey, a young man joined the task, keeping a cellphone cradled to his ear until he left, at the front door of Mx. Sulkowicz's dorm.

It is hard to fathom the effect "Carry That Weight" will have as it proceeds — on Columbia, on Mx. Sulkowicz, on the consciousness of sexual assault on campus, or on the thinking of people who encounter the performance. But it seems certain that the piece has set a very high standard for any future work they'll do as an artist and will also earn them a niche in the history of intensely personal yet aggressively political performance art.

It is so simple: A person with a mattress, refusing to keep their violation private, carrying with them a stark reminder of where it took place. The work Mx. Sulkowicz is making is strict and lean, yet inclusive and open ended, symbolically laden yet drastically physical. All of this determines its striking quality as art, which in turn contributes substantially to its effectiveness as protest.

Columbia Settles With Student Cast as a Rapist in Mattress Art Project

BY KATE TAYLOR | JULY 14, 2017

Editor's Note: The language of this article has been updated to reflect Emma Sulkowicz's use of nonbinary honorifics and pronouns.

IT WAS A PERFORMANCE ART piece that became famous: A person who felt that Columbia University had mishandled their charge of rape against a fellow student turned that anger into their senior arts thesis, a yearlong project in which they carried a 50-pound mattress whenever they were on the Morningside Heights campus.

The individual, Emma Sulkowicz, won national acclaim and was largely embraced by their fellow students, who often helped them carry the burden, which they even brought to a graduation ceremony in May 2015.

The accused man, Paul Nungesser, who was cleared of responsibility in the case by a university disciplinary panel, found himself alternately hounded and ostracized, and condemned at a campus rally and on fliers posted around campus. A month before he and Mx. Sulkowicz received their degrees, he sued Columbia, accusing it of supporting what he called an "outrageous display of harassment and defamation" by giving Mx. Sulkowicz academic credit for their project.

Columbia said late this week that it had reached a settlement with Mr. Nungesser, the terms of which it did not disclose. But the university said in a statement: "Columbia recognizes that after the conclusion of the investigation, Paul's remaining time at Columbia became very difficult for him and not what Columbia would want any of its students to experience. Columbia will continue to review and update its policies toward ensuring that every student — accuser and accused, including those like Paul who are found not responsible — is treated respectfully and as a full member of the Columbia community."

Mr. Nungesser's lawyer, Andrew T. Miltenberg, said it had been important to Mr. Nungesser and his parents that Columbia "take

Paul Nungesser in 2014. He accused Columbia University of enabling a harassment campaign by a fellow student who had accused him of rape. A university disciplinary panel cleared him in 2013 of responsibility in the case.

some steps to ensure that this wouldn't happen again, that this type of experience wouldn't be suffered by someone else." Of the settlement Mr. Miltenberg said: "It's as reasonable of an ending as you can have under these circumstances. Paul still has to live with this, and I suspect he will for a long time."

Mx. Sulkowicz did not respond to a request for comment.

The news of the settlement comes as the Trump administration is revisiting policies on campus sexual assault that the federal Department of Education put in place under President Barack Obama. The policies led the government to investigate many universities and colleges, including Columbia, over their handling of sexual assault cases under the federal law known as Title IX, which prohibits gender discrimination by any school that receives federal funding.

On Thursday, Betsy DeVos, the secretary of education, met with women who said they had been assaulted, with students who had been accused and their families, with higher education officials, and with advocates on both sides of the issue. After the meetings, Ms. DeVos said, "there are lives that have been ruined and lives that are lost in the process," referring to students accused of assault.

But, she said, "We can't go back to the days when allegations were swept under the rug."

Advocates for sexual assault victims expressed some concern on Friday about the settlement of Mr. Nungesser's suit.

"I hope that schools don't interpret this as a sign that they should be cracking down on student activism," said Dana Bolger, a founder of the organization Know Your IX, which is focused on ending sexual violence on college campuses.

She added, "Especially now as we see some retrenchment from the current administration, it's more important than ever that student speech is allowed to thrive on campuses."

Annie E. Clark, the executive director of the group End Rape on Campus, said she was disappointed that Columbia was not more concerned about victims of assaults and that it had not said it was "committed to the process on all sides and that they would support survivors, as well, but we did not see that."

Cynthia Garrett, a co-president of Families Advocating for Campus Equality, which argues that current procedures tilt too heavily in the direction of the accusers, said that the settlement did not make up for what Mr. Nungesser had endured.

"I don't think it will ever compensate him for the loss of that college experience that he deserved because he was innocent," she said.

Janet Halley, a professor at Harvard Law School who has been among the critics of that university's sexual misconduct procedures, said she was not sure what to think of Columbia's promise to review its policies.

"I can't tell from this statement whether they're promising to suppress the speech of someone like Emma Sulkowicz," she said. "If they're saying that they would gag them, then this is an ominous statement."

But Ms. Halley said she thought Columbia had erred in not distancing itself from Mx. Sulkowicz's project and that the university should not have allowed them to carry the mattress at graduation. By doing so, she said, "they explicitly adopted the speech as their own, because the commencement is the utterance, is the speech, of the university itself.

"In those two ways, I think the university very significantly failed in its role, and I regard this announcement as a confession that it thinks that that's the case," she said.

Mx. Sulkowicz accused Mr. Nungesser of anally raping them on the evening of the first day of classes of their sophomore year. He said the sex had been consensual. After Mx. Sulkowicz filed a complaint with the university, a panel found him not responsible. Mx. Sulkowicz filed a police report in 2014, more than a year and a half after the episode, but later stopped talking to investigators, and no charges were brought. Two other women also accused Mr. Nungesser of sexual misconduct, but he was ultimately not found to be responsible in any of the cases.

The experience led Mx. Sulkowicz to begin the performance, which they called "Mattress Performance (Carry That Weight)." Under rules they set for themself, they had to carry the mattress whenever they were on campus until Mr. Nungesser was no longer there.

Mr. Nungesser's lawsuit had been dismissed twice in Federal District Court. Mr. Miltenberg said that, shortly before settlement talks began, he had filed a notice saying that he intended to appeal the case to the United States Court of Appeals for the Second Circuit. The settlement was first reported by the Columbia Daily Spectator, the student newspaper.

Columbia said in its statement that it stood by its finding clearing Mr. Nungesser of any misconduct. It said he had graduated "as a distinguished John Jay Scholar," an honor recognizing "remarkable academic and personal achievements, dynamism, intellectual curiosity, and original thinking," and that he was currently enrolled in film school. Mr. Miltenberg said that Mr. Nungesser, who is from Germany, was living there.

The St. Paul's Rape Case Shows Why Sexual-Assault Laws Must Change

BY EMILY BAZELON | AUG. 26, 2015

IN THE RAPE TRIAL of Owen Labrie, unfolding this month in a county courtroom in Concord, N.H., this much is settled: When Labrie was an 18-year-old senior at the boarding school St. Paul's, he competed with other male students over who could "score with" or "slay" the most girls. In the days before his graduation in June 2014, Labrie invited a girl, then 15, via email to join him for a "senior salute," which could involve anything from kissing to sex. He had a key, passed around by students, to a mechanical room at the school, and the girl went there with him.

The girl testified last week that she and Labrie had sex, though she "said no three times." Labrie, who testified today, denies this. "It wouldn't have been a good move to have sex with this girl," he said. The dispute is a familiar-enough scenario for a rape case. But the fact that it has gone to court is also relatively unusual for a reason that may seem surprising: Labrie's guilt or innocence hinges on the question of consent. This is much less common than you might assume — in fact, in many states, Labrie probably would not face felony charges of sexual assault at all.

The message that "no means no" has been central to the movement to reduce sexual assault on college campuses. "If she doesn't consent, or if she can't consent, it's rape. It's assault," the actor Benicio Del Toro declares in a video released last year by the White House, and featuring President Obama and Vice President Joe Biden. Some schools, in an effort to make rape easier to prove and punish, have shifted the standard of consent to require a showing of active agreement — "yes means yes" as a substitution for "no means no."

But this message often doesn't line up with legal reality. A majority of states still erect a far higher barrier to prosecution and conviction by relying "on the concept of force in defining rape," as the Northwestern University law professor Deborah Tuerkheimer writes in a forthcoming article in The Emory Law Journal. Tuerkheimer finds that in more than half of the 50 states, a judge or jury must find that a person used force to find him or her guilty of rape. The Model Penal Code, created by the American Law Institute in 1962 to influence and standardize criminal lawmaking, also continues to include a force requirement in its definition of rape.

Beginning in the 1970s, reformers pushed states to stop making victims prove that they physically resisted for a rapist to be convicted. But the idea that rape necessarily includes force has persisted — even though it is "woefully out of step with modern conceptions of sex," Tuerkheimer argues. This idea is changing, but slowly. "The trend is in the direction of removing force requirements, and defining sexual assault in reference to a lack of consent, but there are a lot of laggards," she told me.

New Hampshire is among the minority of states that do not require showing force was involved to prove rape. In 1995, the state adopted language providing that a person is guilty of sexual assault if he or she sexually penetrates another person when "the victim indicates by speech or conduct that there is not freely given consent." This explains how the case against Labrie has proceeded — it's the source of the central felony charge against him. And so Labrie's lawyer is trying to convince the jury that the girl did not make her lack of consent clear enough. (The jury also has the option of finding Labrie guilty of the lesser charge of having sex with a 15-year-old, even if she consented, when he was 18. But this is a misdemeanor rather than a felony.)

On cross-examination, the alleged victim conceded that she lifted up her arms so Labrie could take her shirt off and raised her hips so he could pull off her shorts. She also told the police, when they interviewed her soon after the incident, that "other than me saying no to the first part, I don't think he would have known for a fact that I would not want to do that." At trial, she explained, "I wanted to not cause a conflict," and "I felt like I was frozen." Labrie testified, "I thought she was having a great time." He also admitted to wearing a condom, and his former classmates testified earlier this week that he told them he did have sex with the girl. ("I wanted to look good," Labrie said by way of explanation in his own testimony.)

So the crucial question for the jury may well be: Did Labrie know, or should he have known, that the girl did not freely consent? That seems like the right question to ask.

And yet in many cases, consent is still not the test at all. In her article, Tuerkheimer describes a number of such cases around the country. A recent one in Oregon involved a 12-year-old girl who was raped by her father. The girl — who was living with her mother at the time — was visiting her father in his mobile home when he called her into his bedroom, where he was waiting naked, according to the state court of appeals' account. He proceeded to have sex with her, even though she told him that she "didn't want to do it." She also said she did not "put up a fight" because she thought "he would just fight right back."

The father — who sexually abused his daughter several years earlier, too, according to the appeals court — was convicted of rape under an Oregon law that required a showing of "forcible compulsion," which could include "a threat, express or implied, that places a person in fear of immediate or future death or physical injury." But the appeals court reversed his conviction, finding that "nothing in the record suggests that defendant engaged in any force." The court upheld two related convictions the father also appealed, and recognized the history of sexual abuse, saying it "compelled her to submit," but still found this did not qualify, legally speaking, as a threat.

This is chilling and retrograde. And it shows the gap between the definition of rape in many states and the "culture of consent" at universities, Tuerkheimer argues. As she puts it, "On campus, this is rape; off campus, it often is not." The discrepancy, she argues, diminishes the violation of victims outside universities, even though studies show they are actually more vulnerable to sexual assault than college students.

Tuerkheimer and others are pushing to reform state rape laws and the Model Penal Code. As the American Law Institute re-examines the code's sexual-assault provision for the first time since 1962, a heated debate is taking place over how to replace the old language. Should the code follow states like New Hampshire, or go further and adopt the standard of affirmative consent? States including New York are weighing the same question. It's a hard one. Eliminating the force requirement for rape, on the other hand, is a no-brainer.

Victim in New Hampshire Prep School 'Senior Salute' Case Speaks Out

BY CHRISTINE HAUSER | AUG. 30, 2016

A FEMALE STUDENT at an elite prep school in New Hampshire who accused a male senior of rape in 2014 only for him to be convicted of misdemeanor charges revealed her identity on Tuesday in an interview with NBC, saying she hoped to support other victims by discussing the difficulties she has faced, including being shunned when she returned to the school.

"I want everyone to know that I am not afraid or ashamed anymore, and I never should have been," the teenager, Chessy Prout, who was 15 at the time of the assault at St. Paul's School in Concord, said on "Today."

"It's been two years now since the whole ordeal, and I feel ready to stand up and own what happened to me and make sure other people, other girls and boys, don't need to be ashamed, either," she said with her parents at her side.

Ms. Prout said she was attacked in a mechanical room at the school in May 2014. In the trial that ended last August, a senior, Owen Labrie, was cleared of felony sexual assault charges but convicted of misdemeanor charges, including having sex with someone below the age of consent.

Mr. Labrie, now 20, was sentenced to a year in prison and had to register as a sex offender in New Hampshire. He was freed on $15,000 bail pending his appeal, during which he was ordered to comply with a 5 p.m. curfew at his mother's home in Vermont.

The case cast a spotlight on a culture of secret rites and sexual conquest at St. Paul's, including the "senior salute," in which older students tried to engage younger ones in intimate acts: kissing, touching or more.

The trial included details about the tradition, in which a key to the mechanical room on campus was passed around by senior classmates.

Prosecutors said Mr. Labrie had drawn up a list of potential girls for his senior salute, and according to an affidavit, he told the police that he was "trying to be No. 1 in the sexual scoring at St. Paul's School."

Ms. Prout spent days testifying on the stand during the trial, saying that the accused had bitten her during the encounter and that she had told him "no" more than once.

Mr. Labrie said the encounter had been consensual and had stopped short of sex. A statement from his lawyers on Tuesday said, "We remain hopeful that Mr. Labrie will receive a new trial where the full truth of what occurred with be revealed."

In the interview on Tuesday, Ms. Prout described the difficulties of testifying. "It was something that was necessary," she said, "although it was scary."

"I wouldn't be where I am today without having been able to speak up for myself during that time."

She added, "I want other people to feel empowered and just strong enough to be able to say: 'I have the right to my body. I have the right to say no.' "

Ms. Prout said she was upset by how Mr. Labrie's testimony was received by the jury of nine men and three women. "They said that they didn't believe that he did it knowingly, and that frustrated me a lot because he definitely did do it knowingly," she said.

"And the fact that he was still able to pull the wool over a group of people's eyes bothered me a lot and just disgusted me in some way." The aftermath of the trial was also troubling, Ms. Prout said.

She was determined to return to the school, she said, but some male friends refused to speak to her. On one occasion, she said, two senior football players organizing a Powder Puff football game said, " 'We're only directing this at the upper formers because we're not allowed to look at lower formers anymore.' "

She said she was "thinking that that had to be approved by the rector of the school."

"And they let those boys go up there and make a joke about consent and the age."

"I tried my best to go back to my school and try to have a normal life again. But if they're going to treat this topic as a joke, this is not a place I want to be," she added.

Ms. Prout's parents are suing the school for failing to "meet its most basic obligations to protect the children entrusted to its care," The Concord Monitor reported in June, quoting a copy of the filing.

In an emailed statement about Ms. Prout on Tuesday, the school said it "admires her courage and condemns unkind behavior toward her."

It added, "We feel deeply for her and her family."

"We have always placed the safety and well-being of our students first and are confident that the environment and culture of the school have supported that," the school said. "We categorically deny that there ever existed at the school a culture or tradition of sexual assault. However, there's no denying the survivor's experience caused us to look anew at the culture and environment."

Ms. Prout said she was working on a new social media campaign with the nonprofit organization Pave to support victims of sexual assault.

Mr. Labrie was jailed in March after a judge ruled that he had violated his curfew in Vermont. But in May, a judge released Mr. Labrie again on bail.

In Stanford Rape Case, Brock Turner Blamed Drinking and Promiscuity

BY LIAM STACK | JUNE 8, 2016

BROCK TURNER, the former Stanford University student convicted of sexually assaulting an unconscious woman behind a Dumpster on campus, described his actions as the product of a culture of drinking, peer pressure and "sexual promiscuity," according to his courtroom statement.

In a letter he submitted before being sentenced to six months in jail by Judge Aaron Persky of the Santa Clara County Superior Court, obtained by The New York Times, Mr. Turner said: "I am the sole proprietor of what happened on the night that changed these people's lives forever. I would give anything to change what happened."

The case has spurred a national uproar because of a sentence criticized as far too lenient and a statement by the defendant's father complaining that his son's life had been ruined for "20 minutes of action." The judge is also facing a recall effort and has received threats of violence to him and his family, an official said.

The 23-year-old victim read her own statement in court, recounting the horror of finding out details of her attack on the news (she had been intoxicated and could not remember the assault) and having to break the news to her family.

The night the news came out I sat my parents down and told them that I had been assaulted, to not look at the news because it's upsetting, just know that I'm okay, I'm right here, and I'm okay. But halfway through telling them, my mom had to hold me because I could no longer stand up. I was not okay.

Mr. Turner said the events of that night had left him "a changed person." In addition to his six-month jail sentence — far less than the 14-year maximum — he will serve three years' probation and must register as a sex offender. He also lost his swimming scholarship to Stanford.

In his letter, he said the woman had consented to the sexual encounter, even as he admitted "imposing trauma and pain" on her. He repeatedly cited an environment of peer pressure, drinking and promiscuity, factors he said he would use his time on probation to advocate against.

"I want to demolish the assumption that drinking and partying are what make up a college lifestyle," he wrote. "I made a mistake, I drank too much, and my decisions hurt someone."

The woman passionately denounced his interpretation — especially his emphasis on alcohol and promiscuity — in her statement.

"Alcohol is not an excuse," she wrote. "Regretting drinking is not the same as regretting sexual assault," she added. "We were both drunk; the difference is I did not take off your pants and underwear, touch you inappropriately and run away."

The victim's statement went viral after it was published last week by BuzzFeed. It was read live on CNN by the anchor Ashleigh Banfield on Monday. On Wednesday afternoon, Mayor Bill de Blasio of New York said that his wife, Chirlane McCray, and other figures would read the statement from Gracie Mansion in a video posted to his Facebook page.

Why the Stanford Rape Trial Actually Represents Progress

BY EMILY BAZELON | JUNE 9, 2016

IN THE WEEK SINCE he received a six-month jail sentence for committing sexual assault, the former Stanford University student Brock Turner has become a symbol of the rapist who got off easy. But other aspects of the case suggest a different interpretation, signaling that the cultural and legal responses to rape are shifting, in the direction that victims and their supporters have long fought for. Turner's light sentence means that the reform they advocate is incomplete. But his conviction, the punishment he received from Stanford and the public outcry over his sentence all suggest that men who act like Turner have far more reason to think they'll pay a price than they once had.

One day in January 2015, at around 1 a.m., two male Stanford graduate students from Sweden who were riding bicycles spotted Turner, then a 19-year-old freshman, on top of a woman behind a Dumpster outside the Kappa Alpha fraternity house on campus. The graduate students could see that the woman wasn't moving. When they got off their bikes to intervene, Turner tried to run away. They stopped him and called the police. The victim, a college graduate who was 22, was "completely unresponsive," according to the authorities. She was taken to the hospital, where she woke up about three hours later.

Earlier in the evening, she'd gone to a party at the fraternity with her sister. Turner was also there, and they each had several drinks. The victim's blood-alcohol level was about three times the legal limit when it was tested. At some point during the party, she blacked out, and in the hour or so before she was assaulted, she made incoherent calls to her boyfriend and her sister (who'd left the party), which she couldn't remember afterward. She also couldn't remember what happened between her and Turner. His blood-alcohol level was twice the legal limit, and he told the police that though he was drunk, he could "remember everything," according to the police report, and that he'd "consciously decided to engage in the sexual activity with the victim," digitally penetrating her and then thrusting against her with his pants on. He also said she "seemed to enjoy" it — a characterization the victim said she found unforgivable, in a statement she read aloud at Turner's sentencing hearing.

Nonetheless, the case could have ended with Turner's assertions of the woman's consent. "Many campus officials — police and prosecutors, too — wouldn't get past a woman saying 'I don't remember,'" says Deborah Tuerkheimer, a law professor at Northwestern who teaches and writes about rape law. Turner was a star swimmer. The victim had been drinking. He might have been believed. She might have been dismissed or blamed.

And yet at every stage of this case, until the sentencing, it was Turner's account that was discredited. Certain facts help explain why. The victim's vagina was lacerated and had dirt in it, a nurse told her. The graduate students who appeared on the scene could testify to her inability to respond at the moment of the assault. One of them cried while he recounted the incident to the police, saying "it was a very disturbing event" to witness. The victim wasn't verbally protesting or physically struggling, but the graduate students knew something was terribly wrong because she wasn't moving. The prosecutors and the jury saw it the same way when they charged and convicted Turner. Less than two weeks after the incident, he withdrew from Stanford and was banned from the campus — "effectively an expulsion," according to Lisa Lapin, a university spokeswoman.

All of that marks significant progress, in Tuerkheimer's view. She has researched cases in which women have received no justice after reporting that they couldn't consent to sex because they were incapacitated by drinking. Such outcomes reflect a reluctance to hold men accountable when they might have thought, however wrongly, that consent was implied. Blackouts can be especially confounding for courts and campus officials, because people can keep walking and talking even as their memory shuts down. The writer Sarah Hepola, author of "Blackout: Remembering the Things I Drank to Forget," calls this state "spooky, alcohol-induced amnesia." She is careful to say that a person who is unconscious has passed the point of being able to consent to sex, but looking back at her own experience of blackouts, she thinks that for her, "the difference between incapacitated sex and intoxicated sex looked more like a giant question mark."

When a man accused of assault has also been drinking, the courts at times have considered his intoxication a reason to excuse his belief that sex was consensual. At Turner's trial, the jurors were instructed to convict if the defendant knew or reasonably should have known that the victim was too intoxicated to give consent. That's the usual standard. But should the drunkenness of a sexual aggressor factor into evaluating his state of mind? The American Law Institute is currently re-examining the sexual-assault provisions of the Model Penal Code for the first time since 1962. The general rule in criminal law is that recklessness resulting from intoxication does not lessen culpability, but the A.L.I. is considering making an exception to that rule, specifically for rape law. A preliminary proposal acknowledges that this would create a legal "anomaly," giving the hypothetical example of a college student at a frat party who drinks two beers and a shot of whiskey. "Is it sensible to assume," the proposal asks, that "he is aware of a substantial risk that he will commit rape?" At Turner's sentencing hearing, Judge Aaron Persky said a defendant who is intoxicated has "less moral culpability," according to The Guardian.

Yet the outraged reaction to Turner's light sentence — he faced up to 14 years in prison — suggests that it has become increasingly unacceptable to excuse sexual aggression because of drinking. " 'We were both totally out of it' is just not a defense," Kathleen A. Bogle, a sociology and criminal-justice professor at LaSalle University, and Anne M. Coughlin, a law professor at the University of Virginia, argued in Slate two years ago. "It would be unthinkable — wouldn't it? — to acquit killers, kidnappers or thieves for this reason." More than 750,000 people

"Affirmative" or "active" consent varies across states, but it typically requires a verbal or nonverbal "yes" from both parties. Under President Barack Obama, universities used Title IX, the 1972 law requiring universities to protect students from rape and sexual assault, to investigate allegations involving their students.

In 2014, Gov. Andrew M. Cuomo of New York was quick to follow California, ordering the State University of New York to overhaul its sexual assault policies and make affirmative consent mandatory on all 64 campuses. SUNY obliged, but three years later, an appeals court reversed a decision by SUNY Potsdam to expel a student for sexual assault. The court claimed that the university's investigation had been based on hearsay.

In 2015, Indiana University, which defines consent as something that requires sobriety, found that a male student had sexually assaulted a female student who had been drinking. The case was investigated by the university's Title IX office, and the male student was expelled, but in 2016 prosecutors dismissed the case in criminal court, citing insufficient evidence.

Many universities, from public state colleges to the Ivy Leagues, have come under fire for how they have dealt with sexual assault investigations. The Chronicle of Higher Education has tracked the federal government's investigations of colleges' possible mishandling of sexual assault reports. As of Saturday, there were 419 such investigations, of which 350 remained open.

In early July, the education secretary, Betsy DeVos, said she intended to take a hard look at whether the Obama administration's campus rape policies, which jump-started the "affirmative" and "active" consent movement, deprived accused students of their rights.

In an interview with The New York Times, the official appointed to lead the Office of Civil Rights, Candice E. Jackson, said that "90 percent" of sexual assault accusations on campus "fall into the category of 'we were both drunk,' 'we broke up, and six months later I found myself under a Title IX investigation because she just decided that our last time sleeping together was not quite right.' " Ms. Jackson later apologized, calling her remarks "flippant."

Critics of Ms. DeVos say that the Obama-era policies had a positive effect on women on college campuses. Brett Sokolow, the executive director of the Association of Title IX Administrators, says he is playing a "long game."

"Title IX is 45 years old," he said. "It's waxed and waned. It isn't going anywhere. We just have to figure out how to navigate it."

In February, End Rape on Campus, a survivor advocacy organization, created the hashtag #DearBetsy, a reference to the education secretary, and urged the posting of messages on Twitter in support of "sexual assault survivors."

In the past few weeks, Twitter users on all sides of the heated debate began using the hashtag:

#DearBetsy Survivors& advocates feel they are entitled to more time than anyone else got while meeting with you, but they aren't

— NeverGiveUp (@NeverGiveUp1030) Jul. 26, 2017

Thank you, Sec DeVos. The stories of railroaded TIX boys r shameful. Stopping assault DOES NOT REQUIRE EXPELLING INNOCENT BOYS! #DearBetsy

— Jacques Burbank (@JBforjustice) Jul. 28, 2017

@BetsyDeVosED thank you for already making a difference. Student now have a hope and a future BECAUSE of you and @CEJacksonLaw #fairness

— Kay Newman (@cottage_belle), replying to @BetsyDeVosED Jul. 28, 2017

When did feminism become man-hating? Equal rights doesn't mean no rights for men. TIX is for fair treatment. #DearBetsy

— Margaret Valois (@MCVEsquix) Jul. 27, 2017

Mr. Premjee said on Saturday that he was not aware of the national debate or of Ms. DeVos's position on the issue, but added that it sounded like one he would support.

"The key issue here is evidence," he said. "In most sexual assault cases, there's not video evidence like there was in my case. Innocent men are put in prison for that, or are punished, or kicked out of school."

Aziz Ansari Is Guilty.
Of Not Being a Mind Reader.

OPINION | BY BARI WEISS | JAN. 15, 2018

I'M APPARENTLY the victim of sexual assault. And if you're a sexually active woman in the 21st century, chances are that you are, too.

That is what I learned from the "exposé" of Aziz Ansari published last weekend by the feminist website Babe — arguably the worst thing that has happened to the #MeToo movement since it began in October. It transforms what ought to be a movement for women's empowerment into an emblem for female helplessness.

The headline primes the reader to gird for the very worst: "I went on a date with Aziz Ansari. It turned into the worst night of my life." Like everyone else, I clicked.

The victim in this 3,000-word article is called Grace — not her real name — and her experience with Mr. Ansari began at a 2017 Emmys after-party. As recounted by the woman to the reporter Katie Way, she approached him, and they bonded over their admiration of the same vintage camera.

The woman was at the party with someone else, but she and Mr. Ansari exchanged numbers and soon arranged a date in Manhattan.

After arriving at his TriBeCa apartment on the appointed evening — she was "excited," having carefully chosen her outfit after consulting with friends — they exchanged small talk and drank wine. "It was white," she said. "I didn't get to choose and I prefer red, but it was white wine." Yes, we are apparently meant to read the nonconsensual wine choice as foreboding.

They went out to dinner nearby and then returned to Mr. Ansari's apartment. As she tells it, Mr. Ansari was far too eager to get back to his place after he paid for dinner: "Like, he got the check and then it was bada-boom, bada-bing, we're out of there." Another sign of his apparent boorishness.

She complimented Mr. Ansari's kitchen countertops. He then made a move, asking her to sit on top of them. They started kissing. He undressed her and then himself.

In the 30 or so minutes that followed — recounted beat by cringe-inducing beat — they hooked up. Mr. Ansari persistently tried to have penetrative sex with her, and the woman says she was deeply uncomfortable throughout. At various points, she told the reporter, she attempted to voice her hesitation, but Mr. Ansari ignored her signals.

At last, she uttered the word "no" for the first time during their encounter, to Mr. Ansari's suggestion that they have sex in front of a mirror. He responded, " 'How about we just chill, but this time with our clothes on?' "

They dressed, sat on the couch and watched "Seinfeld." She told him, "You guys are all the same." He called her an Uber. She cried on the way home. Fin.

If you are wondering what about this evening constituted the "worst night" of this woman's life, or why it is being framed as a #MeToo story by a feminist website, you probably feel as confused as Mr. Ansari did the next day. "It was fun meeting you last night," he texted.

"Last night might've been fun for you, but it wasn't for me," she responded. "You ignored clear nonverbal cues; you kept going with advances. You had to have noticed I was uncomfortable." He replied with an apology.

Read her text message again.

Put in other words: I am angry that you weren't able to read my mind.

It is worth carefully studying this story. Encoded in it are new yet deeply retrograde ideas about what constitutes consent — and what constitutes sexual violence.

We are told by the reporter that the woman "says she used verbal and nonverbal cues to indicate how uncomfortable and distressed she was." She adds that "whether Ansari didn't notice Grace's reticence or knowingly ignored it is impossible for her to say." We are told that "he wouldn't let her move away from him," in the encounter.

Yet Mr. Ansari, in a statement responding to the account, said that "by all indications" the encounter was "completely consensual."

I am a proud feminist, and this is what I thought while reading the article:

If you are hanging out naked with a man, it's safe to assume he is going to try to have sex with you.

If the failure to choose a pinot noir over a pinot grigio offends you, you can leave right then and there.

If you don't like the way your date hustles through paying the check, you can say, "I've had a lovely evening and I'm going home now."

If you go home with him and discover he's a terrible kisser, say, "I'm out."

If you start to hook up and don't like the way he smells or the way he talks (or doesn't talk), end it.

If he pressures you to do something you don't want to do, use a four-letter word, stand up on your two legs and walk out his door.

Aziz Ansari sounds as if he were aggressive and selfish and obnoxious that night. Isn't it heartbreaking and depressing that men — especially ones who present themselves publicly as feminists — so often act this way in private? Shouldn't we try to change our broken sexual culture? And isn't it enraging that women are socialized to be docile and accommodating and to put men's desires before their own? Yes. Yes. Yes.

But the solution to these problems does not begin with women torching men for failing to understand their "nonverbal cues." It is for women to be more verbal. It's to say, "This is what turns me on." It's to say, "I don't want to do that." And, yes, sometimes it means saying goodbye.

The single most distressing thing to me about this story is that the only person with any agency in the story seems to be Aziz Ansari. The woman is merely acted upon.

All of this put me in mind of another article published this weekend, this one by the novelist and feminist icon Margaret Atwood. "My fundamental position is that women are human beings," she writes.

"Nor do I believe that women are children, incapable of agency or of making moral decisions. If they were, we're back to the 19th century, and women should not own property, have credit cards, have access to higher education, control their own reproduction or vote. There are powerful groups in North America pushing this agenda, but they are not usually considered feminists."

Except, increasingly, they are.

The article in Babe was met with digital hosannas by young feminists who insisted that consent is consent only if it is affirmative, active, continuous and — and this is the word most used — enthusiastic. Consent isn't the only thing they are radically redefining. A recent survey by The Economist/YouGov found that approximately 25 percent of millennial-age American men think asking someone for a drink is harassment. More than a third of millennial men and women say that if a man compliments a woman's looks it is harassment.

To judge from social media reaction, they also see a flagrant abuse of power in this sexual encounter. Yes, Mr. Ansari is a wealthy celebrity with a Netflix show. But he had no actual power over the woman — professionally or otherwise. And lumping him in with the same movement that brought down men who ran movie studios and forced themselves on actresses, or the factory-floor supervisors who demanded sex from female workers, trivializes what #MeToo first stood for.

I'm sorry this woman had this experience. I too have had lousy romantic encounters, as has every adult woman I know. I have regretted these encounters, and not said anything at all. I have regretted them and said so, as she did. And I know I am lucky that these unpleasant moments were far from being anything approaching assault or rape, or even the worst night of my life.

But the response to her story makes me think that many of my fellow feminists might insist that my experience was just that, and for me to define it otherwise is nothing more than my internalized misogyny.

There is a useful term for what this woman experienced on her night with Mr. Ansari. It's called "bad sex." It sucks.

The feminist answer is to push for a culture in which boys and young men are taught that sex does not have to be pursued as if they're in a pornographic film, and one in which girls and young women are empowered to be bolder, braver and louder about what they want. The insidious attempt by some women to criminalize awkward, gross and entitled sex takes women back to the days of smelling salts and fainting couches. That's somewhere I, for one, don't want to go.

Aziz, We Tried to Warn You

OPINION | BY LINDY WEST | JAN. 17, 2018

IN 1975, 42 YEARS before the comedian Aziz Ansari reportedly brought a date home to his apartment and repeatedly tried to initiate sex with her after she told him "next time" and "I don't want to feel forced," Susan Brownmiller published "Against Our Will: Men, Women, and Rape."

"All rape is an exercise in power," Brownmiller wrote in 1975, "but some rapists have an edge that is more than physical." Sometimes, the 1975 text suggests, rapists "operate within an emotional setting or within a dependent relationship that provides a hierarchical, authoritarian structure of its own that weakens a victim's resistance, distorts her perspective and confounds her will." "Against Our Will" has been available in American libraries since its publication, which was in 1975.

Ansari would have been 7 or 8 years old in 1991 when a feminist group at Antioch College fought to establish the school's Sexual Offense Prevention Policy (informally the "Antioch rules" or, more commonly, the "infamous Antioch rules") requiring affirmative and sustained consent throughout all sexual encounters, and he was 10 when "Saturday Night Live" mocked the Antioch rules in a sketch that cast Shannen Doherty as a "Victimization Studies" major.

Also in 1991, Anita Hill testified before the Senate Judiciary Committee, detailing repeated sexual harassment at the hands of her boss, Clarence Thomas, who is still on the Supreme Court. Like Ansari, I, too, was 8 in 1991, and I vividly recall my mother explaining sexual harassment to me in the living room of my childhood home: "For example, a man might say, 'I have a big penis, and I bet you'd like me to —' well, you know." She cut off, disgusted.

In 2008, Jessica Valenti and Jaclyn Friedman edited the anthology "Yes Means Yes!: Visions of Female Sexual Power and a World Without Rape," seven years before Ansari released his own book, "Modern

Aziz Ansari in New York last year.

Romance: An Investigation," in which he explores dating and sex in the digital age.

In the summer of 2014 (perhaps as Ansari was writing his own book), the California Legislature passed a bill requiring "affirmative, conscious, and voluntary agreement to engage in sexual activity," unleashing a debate on the efficacy of "yes means yes" that consumed the blogosphere for months. "Lack of protest or resistance does not mean consent, nor does silence mean consent," the bill stated. Feminist publications covered the issue exhaustively. In October 2014, Ansari appeared on "The Late Show With David Letterman" and declared himself a feminist.

In 2015, two years before Ansari stuck his fingers in a woman's mouth who'd just told him "no, I don't think I'm ready to do this," according to the woman's account, which was published this past weekend, Kate Harding published "Asking for It: The Alarming Rise of Rape Culture — and What We Can Do About It," in which she described sexual assault as "not a 'mistake' but a deliberate decision to treat another person like a soulless object." The same year, Rebecca Traister of New York Magazine argued for the need to look beyond consent to systems of power in an essay titled "The Game Is Rigged: Why Sex That's Consensual Can Still Be Bad."

There is a reflexive tendency, when grappling with stories of sexual misconduct like the accusations leveled at Ansari this past weekend — incidents that seem to exist in that vast gray area between assault and a skewed power dynamic — to point out that sexual norms have changed. This is true. The line between seduction and coercion has shifted, and shifted quickly, over the past few years (the past few months, even). When I was in my 20s, a decade ago, sex was something of a melee. "No means no" was the only rule, and it was still solidly acceptable in mainstream social circles to bother somebody until they agreed to have sex with you. (At the movies, this was called romantic comedy.)

What's not true is the suggestion that complex conversations about consent are new territory, or that men weren't given ample opportunity to catch up.

The books and articles and incidents and perspectives I listed above are nowhere near comprehensive, nor are they perfect, nor are they all in alignment with one another. But they are part of an extensive body of scholarship and activism, and they have been there this whole time for anyone who cared enough to pay attention. You don't have to agree with the Antioch rules to be aware that they exist. You don't have to build a shrine to Brownmiller to internalize the fact that women and femmes are autonomous human beings, many of whom felt dehumanized and unsatisfied by the old paradigm.

The notion of affirmative consent did not fall from space in October 2017 to confound well-meaning but bumbling men; it was built, loudly and painstakingly and in public, at great personal cost to its proponents, over decades. If you're fretting about the perceived overreach of #MeToo, maybe start by examining the ways you've upheld the stigmatization of feminism. Nuanced conversations about consent and gendered socialization have been happening every single day that Aziz Ansari has spent as a living, sentient human on this earth. The reason they feel foreign to so many men is that so many men never felt like they needed to listen. Rape is a women's issue, right? Men don't major in women's studies.

It may feel like the rules shifted overnight, and what your dad called the thrill of the chase is now what some people are calling assault. Unfortunately, no one — even plenty of men who call themselves feminists — wanted to listen to feminist women themselves. We tried to warn you. We wish you'd listened, too.

LINDY WEST is the author of "Shrill: Notes From a Loud Woman" and a contributing opinion writer.

At Yale, Trying Campus Rape in a Court of Law

BY VIVIAN WANG | FEB. 25, 2018

THE DETAILS OF that night in New Haven were not all that different from many others. There was the off-campus party. The alcohol. The attempts the next morning to make sense of the memories that weren't there, and the used condoms that were.

What was different was what came next: the report to the police. The prosecutors pressing charges. And now, the trial.

When Saifullah Khan, 25, stands trial in New Haven this week, accused of raping a fellow Yale student on Halloween of 2015, he will join the ranks of a small, unusual group: men who are accused of sexual assault on campus, and who then hear those accusations aired in a court of law.

There is no log of how many campus rape cases go to trial each year, but experts and victim advocates agree that the number is vanishingly small. The Department of Justice estimates that between 4 percent and 20 percent of female college students who are raped report the attack to law enforcement. Of reported cases, only a fraction lead to arrests, let alone a trial.

The one at Yale, then, might seem like a perfect case to test the fiercely debated question of whether college rape accusations are best handled by internal university panels or by law enforcement. It's a question the secretary of education, Betsy DeVos, has herself raised, in rescinding Obama-era policies on campus sexual assault that demanded schools use lower standards of proof for finding accused students responsible.

Instead, the case has revealed just how difficult it is to separate the two.

Yale, like many other large universities, employs its own police force, which investigated the accusation against Mr. Khan and arrested him; the prosecution is being carried out by the Connecticut state's attorney's office. Mr. Khan's lawyers say the university covertly influenced the police inquiry, working hand-in-glove with officers in a way that has compromised Mr. Khan's right to a fair trial. They argue that Yale, under fire for not taking sexual assault on its campus seriously, blurred the line between school and law enforcement in the name of proving that it did.

As universities across the country face mounting pressure — if not from the federal government, then from public opinion, amid the #MeToo movement — to act on sexual misconduct, that line may become even blurrier.

"This isn't about which institution is better," said Janet Halley, a Harvard Law School professor who has written about the legal implications of Title IX enforcement. "It's about what happens when you put two institutions into the same process and they have different rationalities, different institutional cultures — but above all different rights attached to them.

"This is oil and water flowing in together."

According to an affidavit signed by a Yale police officer, Mr. Khan and his accuser, who is identified only as "the victim," were seniors who lived in the same dormitory. She considered him an acquaintance, the victim said, and they had never been in a romantic relationship.

On Oct. 31, 2015, the victim ate dinner with Mr. Khan, then attended an off-campus party, where Mr. Khan was also present. After the party, the victim and her friends returned to campus to watch the student orchestra's Halloween show, a school tradition.

By that point, the victim said, she had at least four drinks and was so drunk that Yale staff asked her to step out of line after she struggled to pull up her orchestra ticket on her cellphone. When she rejoined the line, her friends had disappeared. Mr. Khan was by her side instead.

They sat together during the show, during which she vomited several times. Afterward, Mr. Khan walked her back to her dorm room, where she vomited again. She said she remembered lying on her bed, fully clothed, and that Mr. Khan lay down next to her.

At some point in the night, she said, she found Mr. Khan on top of her, and she struggled to push him off. When she woke up the next morning, she was naked. There were used condoms on the floor, and bruises on her thighs and knees.

"What you did to me last night was wrong," she told Mr. Khan, according to the affidavit. "You should leave." Mr. Khan replied that she had vomited so much that she had become sober, and that she had consented to sex.

After Mr. Khan left, the victim said, she looked through her phone and found that he had sent messages to her friends on her behalf the night before, declining their invitations to meet up after the show.

The next day, the victim visited Yale's sexual harassment and assault resource center, where an administrator called the police. Officers interviewed Mr. Khan on Nov. 6 and arrested him six days later. He was also suspended from Yale on Nov. 9.

At the heart of defense lawyers' argument is the Yale Police Department, which, like its municipal counterpart, the New Haven Police Department, has full policing powers and responsibilities. But unlike the New Haven Police Department, Mr. Khan's lawyers contend, the Yale force is an arm of the university. Yale's internal sexual misconduct panel uses a lower standard of evidence than the "beyond a reasonable doubt" requirement of the criminal justice system.

In court filings, Mr. Khan's lawyers laid out an extensive list of collaborations between the department and school officials, including a meeting between a lawyer for Yale and an assistant police chief around the time of witness interviews, and the possible disclosure by university administrators of Mr. Khan's confidential educational records to the police without his consent.

All of which, the lawyers said, was detailed in notes that the Yale police hid from prosecutors and defense attorneys, until the very day testimony was supposed to begin last fall. A judge declared a mistrial, delaying the case until this month.

"The fundamental question in this case is whether the Yale Police Department operates in accordance with constitutional duties incumbent on all law enforcement," Mr. Khan's lawyers wrote, "or whether it is a de facto arm of the campus bureaucracy and, vicariously, politics."

The state prosecutor on the case, Michael Pepper, declined to comment, as did a Yale spokesman. Daniel Erwin, a lawyer for Mr. Khan, also declined to comment.

Ms. Halley, the Harvard law professor, said the collision — and alleged collusion — between the Yale and police investigations was inevitable.

University administrators have long worked closely with their campus police forces on issues such as robbery or substance abuse, she said. That the two would work together on sexual assault was a natural outgrowth.

Samantha Harris, vice president of policy research at the Foundation for Individual Rights in Education, a free-speech advocacy group that has criticized the now-rescinded Obama-era guidelines, called the case "Exhibit A" for why universities should leave rape investigations to independent police departments.

"It seems like kind of the worst-case scenario, where the university's processes may have affected the ability of the criminal justice system to function properly," Ms. Harris said.

Yet the case has also illustrated some of the reasons activists say victims avoid the criminal justice system.

The case has dragged on for more than two years, prolonged in no short degree by the mistrial. The plodding pace of prosecutions is a frequently cited deterrent to reporting. The trial has also made the incident far more public than an internal investigation would have. Public court records lay out in stark detail the victim's account of the night, her friends' names, and details such as how much she had to drink and what she was wearing.

Jennifer Long, chief executive officer of AEquitas, a group that advises prosecutors on trying accusations of violence against women, said victims often fear that those details, if publicly disclosed, would invite attacks on their credibility.

The debate around who should handle investigations seems unlikely to fade. Even as Ms. DeVos has permitted universities to more closely align their hearing processes with those the criminal justice system, she has also retained the requirement that schools investigate claims of sexual misconduct, rather than simply hand them off to law enforcement.

As a result, Ms. Halley said of the Yale trial, "all of this was inevitable."

"This may be the tip of an iceberg that we'll see more of," she said. "This is a new frontier of cooperation."

Yale Rape Verdict Shows How 'Yes Means Yes' Can Be Murkier in Court

BY VIVIAN WANG | MARCH 8, 2018

WHEN A JURY in the trial of a Yale college student on rape charges returned a verdict of not guilty on Wednesday, after barely three hours of deliberations, the message seemed clear: Evidence that might warrant punishment from a campus panel was insufficient for a court of law.

At the heart of the trial was the question of whether the complainant could have agreed to have sex with the defendant, Saifullah Khan, 25, on Halloween night in 2015, when the two found themselves in her dorm room after a night filled with alcohol, text messages and conflicting accounts of flirtatious behavior. The complainant was not named in the arrest warrant application.

Had the case gone before Yale's own internal panel, the outcome might have been different. The panel, the University-Wide Committee on Sexual Misconduct, uses a "preponderance of the evidence" standard in determining responsibility, and its members are trained in a notion of consent where only "yes means yes."

But the jurors seemed to have come to the case with a different understanding of what it means to show consent, highlighting the divide between the standards of sexual behavior espoused in freshman orientation programs and campus brochures, and those that operate in courts of law.

One, speaking anonymously after the verdict out of hesitancy to speak for other jurors, said the panel members asked themselves whether there was "enough evidence to show that there could not have been consent. And we couldn't get there."

James Galullo, another juror, said he did not understand the outrage that the verdict had inspired on campus, among students who wrote angry opinion pieces for the campus newspaper or took to social media to denounce the outcome.

Saifullah Khan, who was accused of raping a fellow Yale student on Halloween night in 2015, was declared not guilty on Wednesday after barely three hours of deliberations.

"I just think it's lack of experience in the world," Mr. Galullo, 61, said. "The jurors were all basically middle-aged. They were able to see their way through all the noise."

Alexandra Brodsky, a lawyer at the National Women's Law Center who graduated from Yale College and Yale Law School, said, "Schools have adopted consent as an educational tool, but that sometimes means we end up using words that mean different things in different contexts."

"There are many forms of violence that would be condemned on campus, where a prosecutor would have trouble getting a jury to convict," she added.

But even college students disagree on the language of consent. A 2015 poll by the Kaiser Family Foundation and The Washington Post found that 47 percent of current and recent college students said that someone undressing themselves signaled agreement to further sexual activity; 49 percent said it did not.

Defense lawyers did not necessarily paint a flattering picture of their client, who acknowledged having sex with the woman, despite the fact that she had been drinking to the point of vomiting several times. He also said that he had called his longtime girlfriend, with whom he had an open relationship, from the complainant's bedroom.

But Mr. Khan's lawyers pressed the woman on the witness stand about messages she had sent inviting Mr. Khan to dinner, or writing "lol" — short for "laugh out loud" — the morning after the alleged assault, when she woke up with bruising on her legs. Norman Pattis, one of the defense lawyers, asked if the messages indicated her interest in Mr. Khan. She replied that she spoke to everyone in that manner.

Mr. Pattis also asked about a screenshot that she had sent to Mr. Khan of a Shakespeare sonnet that seemed to imply a romantic interest. She replied that she had been joking; the screenshot was from a popular campus Facebook group, where jokes are often posted.

Dan Erwin, who handled jury selection for the defense, said that they had favored "older jurors, 30 to middle-age" because "there was a seriousness about them insofar as none of them accepted, condoned or denied the existence of misconduct, harassment or assault, but they all seriously engaged with the need for due process."

The juror who spoke anonymously said that the panel had not focused on the banter or on Mr. Pattis's suggestion that the woman's Halloween costume had been too sexy. Instead, the jurors focused on evidence like security camera footage that showed the complainant and Mr. Khan walking back to her dorm room. The complainant had testified that the footage showed her so drunk that she was unable to support herself, her leg dragging behind her.

"We looked at and we looked at and we looked at that video of them walking," the juror said. "We could not see her leg dragging. We could not see her eyes shut. We could not see what she said."

Mr. Galullo said the rigorous standard of proof required, coupled with the length of Mr. Khan's possible prison sentence, weighed heavily upon him.

"We wanted to really be sure that he was guilty," he said. "These kids went through a lot. It was really very, very sad. You had tears in your eyes — for both of them."

Mr. Khan may still face a hearing at Yale. He was suspended by the university shortly before he was arrested and charged, and his lawyers said that Yale's disciplinary hearing had been delayed pending the criminal trial. That panel would only have to determine that it was "more likely than not" that he was in the wrong to find him responsible.

Mr. Khan's lawyers are seeking to have him reinstated. A university spokesman declined to confirm or deny the existence of an internal complaint.

Several experts agreed that the distance between campus and criminal understandings of permissible sexual conduct may continue to widen, especially as conversations about sex and power continue to evolve.

While juries must interpret legal definitions of rape, students and administrators have increasingly sought to define "ethical sex," said Vanessa Grigoriadis, author of a book on campus consent policies and a contributing editor at The New York Times Magazine. Unlike criminal courts, Ms. Grigoriadis said, campus communities are quicker to denounce sexual encounters that are "immoral but not criminal."

Jaclyn Friedman, a consent educator and author, said that in the end, "Consent is not a legalistic construction. It gets translated into law, and should be reflected in our laws, but it is actually a moral value."

CHERYL P. WEINSTOCK, KRISTIN HUSSEY and **GRAHAM AMBROSE** contributed reporting.

Glossary

affirmative consent A knowing, voluntary and mutual decision among all participants to engage in sexual activity, given by explicit words or actions.

amicus Someone who is not a party to a legal case who assists a court by offering information about the case.

assault A physical attack.

bystander A person who is present at an event or incident but does not take part.

coercion The practice of persuading someone to do something by using force or threats.

consent Permission for something to happen.

education secretary The head of the United States Department of Education.

incapacitated Deprived of strength, weakened. An individual who is incapacitated by alcohol and/or drugs both voluntary and involuntarily consumed cannot give consent.

mandatory reporting A term used to describe the legislative requirement for select groups to report suspected cases of abuse to authorities.

no means no An antirape slogan that emphasizes sexual consent.

oversexualization The excessive sexualization of a person or group.

rape Unlawful sexual activity carried out forcibly or under threat of injury against the will of a person or with someone under a certain age.

rape culture An environment whose prevailing social attitudes result in the normalizing or trivializing of sexual assault and abuse.

sex positive Having or promoting an open, tolerant or progressive attitude towards sex and sexuality.

sexual misconduct A broad term used to describe any unwelcome behavior of a sexual nature that is committed without consent or by some kind of force.

stalking Engaging in harassing, threatening or unwanted behavior that would cause a reasonable person to fear for their safety.

Title IX The amendment that prohibits discrimination in education on the basis of sex. It states: "No person in the United States shall, on the basis of sex, be excluded from participation in, be denied the benefits of, or be subjected to discrimination under any education program or activity receiving federal financial assistance."

Media Literacy Terms

"Media literacy" refers to the ability to access, understand, critically assess and create media. The following terms are important components of media literacy, and they will help you critically engage with the articles in this title.

angle The aspect of a news story that a journalist focuses on and develops.

attribution The method by which a source is identified or by which facts and information are assigned to the person who provided them.

balance Principle of journalism that both perspectives of an argument should be presented in a fair way.

bias A disposition of prejudice in favor of a certain idea, person or perspective.

byline Name of the writer, usually placed between the headline and the story.

caption Identifying copy for a picture; also called a legend or cutline.

column A type of story that is a regular feature, often on a recurring topic, written by the same journalist, generally known as a columnist.

commentary A type of story that is an expression of opinion on recent events by a journalist generally known as a commentator.

credibility The quality of being trustworthy and believable, said of a journalistic source.

critical review A type of story that describes an event or work of art, such as a theater performance, film, concert, book, restaurant, radio or television program, exhibition or musical piece, and offers critical assessment of its quality and reception.

editorial Article of opinion or interpretation.

fake news A fictional or made-up story presented in the style of a legitimate news story, intended to deceive readers; also commonly used to criticize legitimate news because of its perspective or unfavorable coverage of a subject.

feature story Article designed to entertain as well as to inform.

headline Type, usually 18 point or larger, used to introduce a story.

human interest story A type of story that focuses on individuals and how events or issues affect their life, generally offering a sense of relatability to the reader.

impartiality Principle of journalism that a story should not reflect a journalist's bias and should contain balance.

intention The motive or reason behind something, such as the publication of a news story.

interview story A type of story in which the facts are gathered primarily by interviewing another person or persons.

inverted pyramid A method of writing a story using facts in order of importance, beginning with a lead and then gradually adding paragraphs in order of relevance from most interesting to least interesting.

motive The reason behind something, such as the publication of a news story or a source's perspective on an issue.

news story An article or style of expository writing that reports news, generally in a straightforward fashion and without editorial comment.

op-ed An opinion piece that reflects a prominent individual's opinion on a topic of interest.

paraphrase The summary of an individual's words, with attribution, rather than a direct quotation of their exact words.

plagiarism An attempt to pass another person's work as one's own without attribution.

quotation The use of an individual's exact words indicated by the use of quotation marks and proper attribution.

reliability The quality of being dependable and accurate, said of a journalistic source.

rhetorical device Technique in writing intending to persuade the reader or communicate a message from a certain perspective.

source The origin of the information reported in journalism.

style A distinctive use of language in writing or speech; also a news or publishing organization's rules for consistent use of language with regards to spelling, punctuation, typography and capitalization, usually regimented by a house style guide.

tone A manner of expression in writing or speech.

Media Literacy Questions

1. Identify the various sources cited in the article "At the College That Pioneered the Rules on Consent, Some Students Want More" (on page 148). How does the journalist attribute information to each of these sources in the article? How effective are the journalist's attributions in helping the reader identify the sources?

2. In "Sex Ed Lesson: 'Yes Means Yes,' but It's Tricky" (on page 21), Jennifer Medina directly quotes Shafia Zaloom. What are the strengths of the use of a direct quote as opposed to a paraphrase? What are its weaknesses?

3. Compare the headlines of "The Challenge of Defining Rape" (on page 14) and "When Yes Means Yes" (on page 129). Which is a more compelling headline, and why? How could the less compelling headline be changed to better draw the reader's interest?

4. What type of story is "Who Is the Victim in the Anna Stubblefield Case?" (on page 33)? Can you identify another article in this collection that is the same type of story?

5. Does Kate Taylor demonstrate the journalistic principle of impartiality in her article "Columbia Settles With Student Cast as a Rapist in Mattress Art Project" (on page 170)? If so, how did she do so? If not, what could she have included to make her article more impartial?

6. The article "Aziz, We Tried to Warn You" (on page 196) is an example of an op-ed. Identify how Lindy West's attitude and tone help convey her opinion on the topic.

7. Does "At Yale, Trying Campus Rape in a Court of Law" (on page 200) use multiple sources? What are the strengths of using multiple sources in a journalistic piece? What are the weaknesses of relying heavily on one source?

8. "In a Mattress, a Lever for Art and Political Protest" (on page 165) is an example of a critical review. What is the purpose of a critical review? Do you feel this article achieved that purpose?

9. "#MenToo" (on page 121) is an example of an interview. What are the benefits of providing readers with direct quotes of an interviewed subject's speech? Is the subject of an interview always a reliable source?

10. What is the intention of the article "The St. Paul's Rape Case Shows Why Sexual-Assault Laws Must Change" (on page 174)? How effectively does it achieve its intended purpose?

11. Analyze the authors' reporting in "Hooking Up at an Affirmative-Consent Campus? It's Complicated" (on page 131) and "Campus Sex … With a Syllabus" (on page 39). Do you think one journalist is more impartial in their reporting than the other? If so, why do you think so?

12. Identify each of the sources in "Betsy DeVos Reverses Obama-era Policy on Campus Sexual Assault Investigations" (on page 112) as a primary source or a secondary source. Evaluate the reliability and credibility of each source. How does your evaluation of each source change your perspective on this article?

13. Often, as news on a particular subject develops over time, a journalist's attitude toward the subject may change. Compare "The St. Paul's Rape Case Shows Why Sexual-Assault Laws Must Change" (on page 174) and "Why the Stanford Rape Trial Actually Represents Progress" (on page 183), both by Emily Bazelon. Did new information discovered between the publication of these two articles change Bazelon's perspective on sexual-assault laws?

14. "Making Consent Cool" (on page 99) features a chart containing the results of two open-response surveys. What does this chart add to the article?

15. "45 Stories of Sex and Consent on Campus" (on page 66) contains multiple primary source accounts of individual experiences with navigating consent on college campuses. What is the intention of the article? How effectively does it achieve its intended purpose?

16. The article "Judge Drops Rape Case Against U.S.C. Student, Citing Video Evidence" (on page 187) includes tweets. What do the tweets add to the article? Are they effective?

17. Identify the various sources cited in the article "Betsy DeVos Ends a Campus Witch Hunt" (on page 118). How does Bret Stephens attribute information to each of these sources in his article? How effective are his attributions in helping the reader identify their sources?

Citations

All citations in this list are formatted according to the Modern Language Association's (MLA) style guide.

BOOK CITATION

NEW YORK TIMES EDITORIAL STAFF, THE. *Defining Sexual Consent: Where the Law Falls Short*. New York: New York Times Educational Publishing, 2019.

ONLINE ARTICLE CITATIONS

ALANI, HANNAH. "Judge Drops Rape Case Against U.S.C. Student, Citing Video Evidence." *The New York Times*, 5 Aug. 2017, https://www.nytimes.com /2017/08/05/us/usc-rape-case-dropped-video-evidence.html.

BATES, LAURA. "The Trouble With Sex Robots." *The New York Times*, 17 Jul. 2017, www.nytimes.com/2017/07/17/opinion/sex-robots-consent.html.

BAZELON, EMILY. "Hooking Up at an Affirmative-Consent Campus? It's Complicated." *The New York Times*, 21 Oct. 2014, www.nytimes.com /2014/10/26/magazine/hooking-up-at-an-affirmative-consent-campus-its -complicated.html.

BAZELON, EMILY. "The St. Paul's Rape Case Shows Why Sexual-Assault Laws Must Change." *The New York Times*, 26 Aug. 2015, www.nytimes.com /2015/08/26/magazine/the-st-pauls-rape-case-shows-why-sexual-assault -laws-must-change.html.

BAZELON, EMILY. "Why the Stanford Rape Trial Actually Represents Progress." *The New York Times*, 9 Jun. 2016, www.nytimes.com/2016/06/09 /magazine/why-the-stanford-rape-conviction-actually-represents -progress.html.

BENNETT, JESSICA. "Campus Sex … With a Syllabus." *The New York Times*, 9 Jan. 2016, www.nytimes.com/2016/01/10/fashion/sexual-consent-assault -college-campuses.html.

BENNETT, JESSICA. "When Saying 'Yes' Is Easier Than Saying 'No.'" *The New*

York Times, 16 Dec. 2017, www.nytimes.com/2017/12/16/sunday-review /when-saying-yes-is-easier-than-saying-no.html.

CHOKSHI, NIRAJ. "Eric Schneiderman, Consent and Domestic Violence." *The New York Times*, 8 May 2018, www.nytimes.com/2018/05/08/nyregion /consent-sexual-assault-rough-sex.html.

DOMINUS, SUSAN. "Getting to 'No.' " *The New York Times*, 22 Dec. 2014, www .nytimes.com/2014/12/07/magazine/getting-to-no.html.

FAURE, VALENTINE. "Can an 11-Year-Old Girl Consent to Sex?" *The New York Times*, 5 Oct. 2017, www.nytimes.com/2017/10/05/opinion/sex-consent-france.html.

GRIGORIADIS, VANESSA. "Sex at Wesleyan: What's Changed, What Hasn't? An Alumna Asks." *The New York Times*, 25 Aug. 2017, www.nytimes.com /2017/08/25/style/wesleyan-sex-rules.html.

GRIGORIADIS, VANESSA. "What the Weinstein Effect Can Teach Us About Campus Sexual Assault." *The New York Times*, 25 Nov. 2017, www.nytimes .com/2017/11/15/opinion/campus-sexual-assault-weinstein.html.

HAUSER, CHRISTINE. "Victim in New Hampshire Prep School 'Senior Salute' Case Speaks Out." *The New York Times*, 31 Aug. 2016, https://www.nytimes .com/2016/08/31/us/chessy-prout-sexual-assault-victim-of-owen-labrie-at -new-hampshire-school-speaks-out.html.

KEENAN, SANDY. "Affirmative Consent: Are Students Really Asking?" *The New York Times*, 28 Jul. 2015, www.nytimes.com/2015/08/02/education /edlife/affirmative-consent-are-students-really-asking.html.

KIMMEL, MICHAEL, AND GLORIA STEINEM. " 'Yes' Is Better Than 'No.' " *The New York Times*, 4 Sept. 2014, www.nytimes.com/2014/09/05/opinion /michael-kimmel-and-gloria-steinem-on-consensual-sex-on-campus.html.

KITROEFF, NATALIE. "Making Consent Cool." *The New York Times*, 7 Feb. 2014, www.nytimes.com/2014/02/09/education/edlife/students-advocate-for -consensual-sex.html.

MCMAHAN, JEFF, AND PETER SINGER. "Who Is the Victim in the Anna Stubblefield Case?" *The New York Times*, 3 Apr. 2017, www.nytimes.com/2017/04/03 /opinion/who-is-the-victim-in-the-anna-stubblefield-case.html.

MEDINA, JENNIFER. "Sex Ed Lesson: 'Yes Means Yes,' but It's Tricky." *The New York Times*, 15 Oct. 2014, www.nytimes.com/2015/10/15/us/california -high-schools-sexual-consent-classes.html.

THE NEW YORK TIMES. "45 Stories of Sex and Consent on Campus." *The New York Times*, 10 May 2018, www.nytimes.com/interactive/2018/05/10/style /sexual-consent-college-campus.html.

THE NEW YORK TIMES. "When Yes Means Yes." *The New York Times*, 8 Sept. 2014, www.nytimes.com/2014/09/09/opinion/california-lawmakers-redefine-campus-sexual-assault.html.

PÉREZ-PEÑA, RICHARD, AND WALT BOGDANICH. "In Florida Student Assaults, an Added Burden on Accusers." *The New York Times*, 14 Sept. 2014, www.nytimes.com/2014/09/15/us/in-florida-student-assaults-an-added-burden-on-accusers.html.

ROSENBERG, TINA. "Equipping Women to Stop Campus Rape." *The New York Times*, 30 May 2018, www.nytimes.com/2018/05/30/opinion/women-stop-campus-rape.html.

ROSMAN, KATHERINE. "At the College That Pioneered the Rules on Consent, Some Students Want More." *The New York Times*, 24 Feb. 2018, www.nytimes.com/2018/02/24/style/antioch-college-sexual-offense-prevention-policy.html.

ROSMAN, KATHERINE. "On the Front Line of Campus Sexual Misconduct." *The New York Times*, 26 Sept. 2015, www.nytimes.com/2015/09/27/fashion/on-the-front-line-of-campus-sexual-misconduct.html.

SALAM, MAYA. "Consent in the Digital Age: Can Apps Solve a Very Human Problem?" *The New York Times*, 2 Mar. 2018, www.nytimes.com/2018/03/02/technology/consent-apps.html.

SAUL, STEPHANIE, AND KATE TAYLOR. "Betsy DeVos Reverses Obama-Era Policy on Campus Sexual Assault Investigations." *The New York Times*, 22 Sept. 2017, www.nytimes.com/2017/09/22/us/devos-colleges-sex-assault.html.

SHULEVITZ, JUDITH. "Regulating Sex." *The New York Times*, 27 Jun. 2015, www.nytimes.com/2015/06/28/opinion/sunday/judith-shulevitz-regulating-sex.html.

SMITH, ROBERTA. "In a Mattress, a Lever for Art and Political Protest." *The New York Times*, 21 Sept. 2014, www.nytimes.com/2014/09/22/arts/design/in-a-mattress-a-fulcrum-of-art-and-political-protest.html.

STACK, LIAM. "In Stanford Rape Case, Brock Turner Blamed Drinking and Promiscuity." *The New York Times*, 8 Jun. 2016, www.nytimes.com/2016/06/09/us/brock-turner-blamed-drinking-and-promiscuity-in-sexual-assault-at-stanford.html.

STEPHENS, BRET. "Betsy DeVos Ends a Campus Witch Hunt." *The New York Times*, 8 Sept. 2017, www.nytimes.com/2017/09/08/opinion/betsy-devos-title-iv.html.

TAYLOR, KATE. "Columbia Settles With Student Cast as a Rapist in Mattress

Art Project." *The New York Times*, 14 Jul. 2017, https://www.nytimes
.com/2017/07/14/nyregion/columbia-settles-with-student-cast-as-a-rapist
-in-mattress-art-project.html.

URBINA, IAN. "The Challenge of Defining Rape." *The New York Times*, 11 Oct.
2014, www.nytimes.com/2014/10/12/sunday-review/being-clear-about
-rape.html.

WANG, VIVIAN. "Yale Rape Verdict Shows How 'Yes Means Yes' Can Be Murkier
in Court." *The New York Times*, 8 Mar. 2018, www.nytimes.com/2018
/03/08/nyregion/yale-rape-verdict-consent-not-guilty-jurors.html.

WANG, VIVIAN. "At Yale, Trying Campus Rape in a Court of Law." *The New York
Times*, 25 Feb. 2018, www.nytimes.com/2018/02/25/nyregion/yale
-campus-rape-trial.html.

WEISS, BARI. "Aziz Ansari Is Guilty. Of Not Being a Mind Reader." *The New
York Times*, 15 Jan. 2015, www.nytimes.com/2018/01/15/opinion/aziz
-ansari-babe-sexual-harassment.html.

WEST, LINDY. "Aziz, We Tried to Warn You." *The New York Times*, 17 Jan. 2018,
www.nytimes.com/2018/01/17/opinion/aziz-ansari-metoo-sex.html.

WILLIAMS, ALEX. "#MenToo." *The New York Times,* 27 Feb. 2018, www
.nytimes.com/interactive/2018/02/27/style/me-too-men-consent
-pledge.html.

WINERIP, MICHAEL. "Stepping Up to Stop Sexual Assault." *The New York Times*,
7 Feb. 2014, www.nytimes.com/2014/02/09/education/edlife
/stepping-up-to-stop-sexual-assault.html.

Index

This book is current up until the time of printing. For the most up-to-date reporting, visit www.nytimes.com.

224 DEFINING SEXUAL CONSENT